Mar. Edmons

A History of All the Real and Threatened Invasions of England

Mar. Edmons

A History of All the Real and Threatened Invasions of England

ISBN/EAN: 9783742857224

Manufactured in Europe, USA, Canada, Australia, Japa

Cover: Foto ©ninafisch / pixelio.de

Manufactured and distributed by brebook publishing software (www.brebook.com)

Mar. Edmons

A History of All the Real and Threatened Invasions of England

A

HISTORY

OF ALL THE

INVASIONS OF ENGLAND,

&c. &c. &c.

Price Four Shillings, in Boards.

A

HISTORY

OF ALL THE REAL AND THREATENED

INVASIONS OF ENGLAND,

FROM

The Landing of JULIUS CÆSAR, to the present Period.

GIVING

A succinct Account of the several Parties,
That either excited, or suppressed the various Commotions,

CONCLUDING WITH

A View of the present State of Affairs.

DEDICATED TO THE

LORD LIEUTENANTS

OF THE COUNTIES OF GREAT BRITAIN.

TO WHICH IS ADDED,

An APPENDIX,

CONTAINING

A MODE OF DEFENDING THE KINGDOM,

WITH AN EPITOME OF

MILITARY HORSEMANSHIP,

AND

GENERAL TACTICS:

TAKEN FROM

Edmonds, Mar. Saxe, Lloyd, Pembroke, Simes,
and others, the most respectable Authors.

"Children, I must now warn you for clouds and storms. Fac—
[ ] on every side, and threaten the tranquility of your native
 But whatever happen, do you faithfully honour and obey
NCE, and ADHERE TO THE CROWN."
Sir T. Windham's Deathbed Advice, in 1636, to his Children.

WINDSOR:
PRINTED FOR, AND SOLD BY, C. KNIGHT.
SOLD ALSO IN LONDON, BY J. WALKER, PATERNOSTER-ROW;
W. STEWART, AND W. OWEN, PICCADILLY.

1794.

TO THE
LORD LIEUTENANTS
OF THE
COUNTIES OF GREAT BRITAIN.

MY LORDS,

THE zeal, promptitude, and liberality, which your Lordships have manifested, on the present important crisis, emboldens me to believe, that however feeble my attempt to emulate your Lordships, in your laudable exertions to defend our GLORIOUS CONSTITUTION, you will rather regard the design, than the ability, with which it has been executed.

CONSCIOUS of my incompetence to do ample justice to the task I have assumed; yet, confident in the rectitude of my intentions, I would crave permission to submit the following Sheets to your Lordships' fostering care and protection; and, to subscribe myself, with due deference and respect,

Your Lordships'

Most devoted

humble Servant,

THE AUTHOR.

WINDSOR,
May 29th, 1794.

INTRODUCTION.

AT a time when the kingdom is agitated by Domestic Conspiracy, as well as Foreign Hostility; it surely becomes the duty of every Loyal Briton, in whatever station Providence may have placed him, to exert his utmost endeavours to avert the threatened Calamities; and to preserve inviolate, the inestimable blessings of our happy Constitution.

When Republican Doctrines have been disseminated, and embraced with a degree of enthusiasm, on the one side; and unqualified submission to Monarchical Government, held forth, by some, on the other; it may not be amiss to shew the errors of both parties, by a faithful display of Historical Facts; and by the examples of Loyalty, Patriotism, and Bravery, that will here be found, to excite and cherish those laudable sentiments. With this view, but more particularly to exhibit the certain ruin, that is the never-failing consequence of a licentious and ungovernable spirit, the present Work has been undertaken; from a perusal of which it is presumed, that every impartial reader will perceive how much the interest and the happiness of the *Governors*, and the

Governed,

Governed, depend on their mutual good will and attachment to each other.

We shall also learn, that the reciprocal advantages resulting from hence, must not be held too lightly; or, the loss of them risked, by a too confident security, or too great a remissness, in not being, at all times, properly prepared, to defend our King, to guard our Liberties, and to protect our Property, against the contingent events of intestine commotion; the possible treachery of our allies; or, the envious assaults of avowed enemies.

We shall not further anticipate the reader's remarks, otherwise than to observe, that in the Military Part of our Work, we have selected such passages, and from such authorities, as we judged might render it not an unpleasing, nor an unuseful Companion to the Subaltern Officers of the Army, during their encampments.

As, before the period of Julius Cæsar's Invasion, all historical events, relative to Great Britain, are involved in obscurity, we have commenced at once with that accomplished Conqueror's expedition into this country.

CONTENTS.

CONTENTS.

PAGE

DEDICATION
Introduction

CHAP. I.

Of the Romans	1
Julius Cæsar's First Invasion	ibid
Cæsar's Second Invasion	7
Augustus's Intended Invasion	12
Caligula's Threatened Invasion	ibid
Claudius's Invasion	14

CHAP. II.

Invasion of the Saxons	18
Abject State of the Britons	20

CHAP. III.

Invasion of the Danes	29
Invasions in Alfred the Great's Reign	36

CHAP. IV.

Norwegian and Norman Invasions	50
Norwegian Invasion	51
Norman Invasion	54

CHAP. V.

	PAGE
Of the French and Spanish early Attempts, at Invasion	69
Spanish Armada	73
Attempts of Philip of Spain to invade Britain	86

CHAP. VI.

Of the Navy, of the Militia, and of the Dutch Invasion	91
Dutch Invasion	97

CHAP. VII.

Duke of Monmouth's Invasion	100

CHAP. VIII.

Invasion of the Prince of Orange, and the Establishment of the Revolution	103

CHAP. IX.

Invasion of Ireland, by James, and an Attempt at the Invasion of England, by Lewis XIV.	113

CHAP. X.

Second Attempt of Lewis XIV. to invade England	124

CHAP XI.

Third Attempt at Invasion, by Lewis XIV.	132

CHAP. XII.

Of the threatened Invasion from Spain, in 1715; from Sweden, in 1717; from Spain, in 1718; and of a Conspiracy to promote an Insurrection, and Invasion, in 1722	139
Attempt of Sweden, in 1717	140
Of the Attempt of Spain, in 1718	143
Conspiracy, in 1722, to favour an Invasion	147

CHAP. XIII.

Projected Invasion, in 1743, by France	152

CHAP. XIV.

	PAGE
Rebellion in 1745, and the Menaced Invasion of France, in 1755, 1756, 1758, and 1759	157
Rebellion, in 1745	ibid
Menaced Invasion, in 1755, and 1756	160
Ditto, in 1758, and 1759	164

CHAP. XV.

Preparations in 1779, and 1782, against Invasion	175

CHAP. XVI.

PRESENT STATE OF AFFAIRS.	179
Strictures on the Opposition to Voluntary Subscriptions	182
Suspension of the Habeas Corpus Act, justifiable upon Precedent, as well as Expedience	185

APPENDIX.

Introductory Remarks on the Defence of the Nation	1
Edmonds' Answers to Queries, respecting the Landing of an Enemy, with his proposed means of defending every part of the Kingdom	3
General Lloyd's opinion on Invasions, and his plan of Defence	8
Lord Bolingbroke's Observations on Invasions	21
HORSMANSHIP, &c.	23
On Sitting the Horse Properly	24
On Suppling Horses, with Men upon them	26
Of Working in Hand	28
Of the Head to the Wall, and the Croup to the Wall	ibid
The Trot	31
Reining back,—and of Moving forwards immediately after	33
To make Horses stand Fire	34
To learn Horses to leap over Ditches, &c.	35
To accustom Horses to swim	36
To cure Restivenesses, &c	ibid
Farriery, &c.	39
Shoeing	40
Miscellaneous Remarks, concerning Cavalry	41
CURSORY HINTS ON TACTICS	43

	PAGE
Discipline	43
New Mode of Forming a Line	44
New Order of Battle	ibid
Of the power of Music in Military Evolutions	45
Of Cavalry	46
To Harrass an invading Army on its March	47
On the Denfity, or Clofenefs of a body of Troops	ibid
Of a Retreat	ibid
English Courage	48
Conclusion	ibid

HISTORY
OF ALL THE
INVASIONS, &c.

CHAP. I.

INVASIONS of the ROMANS.

JULIUS CÆSAR'S FIRST INVASION.

THE first invasion of Britain, by Cæsar, seems, by his own account, to have been rather intended as a partial, than a decisive one; for he says, speaking of himself in the third person,

"Though the time of the year would not permit him to finish the war, yet he thought it would be worth his while to make an expedition thither, only to view the island, to learn the nature of the inhabitants, to be acquainted with their coasts, their ports and creeks, to which the Gauls were almost strangers; for they were seldom visited by any but merchants, who were unacquainted with all the country, except the coasts, and those parts which were opposite to the Gauls. Accordingly, having summoned a council of merchants from "all

"all parts, he could neither be informed of the extent of the island,—what nation,—and how powerful the inhabitants were;—how well they understood the art of war,—what customs they were governed by,—nor how considerable a navy their ports were capable of receiving."

Cæsar, not discouraged by this want of proper intelligence, dispatched C. Volusenus, a tribune of his army, in a galley, to reconnoitre the British coasts, and make such observations as might be of service in the expedition. He, after a five days cruize, returned, and made a report to his commander, of what he had seen.

Some of the British states being informed of Cæsar's great preparations to invade them, and dreading the impending danger, sent ambassadors to him into Gaul, offering to submit to the Romans, and to give hostages for their fidelity. These envoys were graciously received, hospitably entertained, and sent back in company with Comius, as deputy from Cæsar, to the different British kingdoms. Comius, a Briton by birth, but much in Cæsar's favour, was, however, imprudently seized upon, the moment he landed, and imprisoned by his countrymen, who were exasperated *at his attachment to a foreigner and an enemy.*

Cæsar having drawn together his forces, embarked his infantry in eighty, and his cavalry in eighteen transport ships; and set sail from Morini, or Picardy, about one in the morning, on the 26th of August, in the year of the world 3917, and fifty-five years before Christ.

About ten o'clock the same morning, the ships, with the infantry, arrived off Dover; when Cæsar found the cliffs lined with armed Britons, who, from the nature of the place, could oppose his landing with advantage; he

therefore

therefore ordered the ships to cast anchor, called a council of war, gave proper directions to his officers, and, at about four o'clock in the afternoon, again weighed anchor, in order to find a more plain and easy shore; which, after having sailed about eight miles to the northward, he discovered at a place now called Deal. The Britons, guessing his intent, dispatched their chariots and horsemen first, and followed with the rest of the army as expeditiously as possible, in order to oppose the landing of the Romans; which, says Cæsar, "We found it very difficult to "effect, for many reasons; because our ships being heavy, "required a considerable depth of water; and our sol- "diers, while their hands were employed, and loaded "with heavy armour, were, at the same time, to encoun- "ter the waves and the enemy, in a place they were not "acquainted with; whereas, the Britons, either standing "upon dry land, or sallying a little way into the water "in those places they knew to be shallow, having the free "use of all their limbs, could boldly cast their darts, and "spur their horses forward, who were inured to that "kind of combat; which disadvantage so discouraged the "Romans, who were strangers to this way of fighting, "that they did not appear so chearful and eager to engage "the enemy, as in their former conflicts on dry land.

"Cæsar perceiving this, gave orders that the gallies, "a nimble sort of shipping the enemy had never seen, "should advance a little before the rest of the navy, and "row along, with their broadsides towards the shore, "that they might more conveniently force the Britons to "retire from the water side, by their slings, engines, and "arrows, which did the Romans considerable service; "for the Britons, being surprised at the make of our "gallies, the motion of our oars and engines, began to "give ground.

"But

"But the standard-bearer of the tenth legion, perceiv-
"ing our men were unwilling to venture into the sea,
"having first invoked the gods for success, cried out
"aloud,—My fellow soldiers! unless you will forsake
"your eagle, and suffer it to fall into the hands of the
"enemy, advance! for my part, I am resolved to per-
"form my duty to the commonwealth and my general.
"Having said this, he immediately leaped over-board,
"and advanced the eagle towards the Britons; where-
"upon the soldiers, encouraging each other to prevent so
"signal a disgrace, followed his example, which those
"in the next ships perceiving, did the like, and pressed
"forward to the enemy.

"The conflict was sharply maintained on both sides;
"though the Romans, not being able to keep their ranks,
"obtain firm footing, or follow their particular standards,
"leaping out of several ships, and joining the first ensign
"they met with, were in great confusion. But the
"Britons, who were well acquainted with the shallows,
"when they saw us descend in small numbers from our
"ships, spurred their horses into the water, set upon our
"men, incumbered and unprepared to receive them; and
"some surrounded us with their numbers, in one place,
"whilst others flanked us where we lay most open in
"another. This, Cæsar observing, he caused the long-
"boats and smaller vessels to be manned; and, where oc-
"casion required, sent them to assist their fellows; thus
"our foremost ranks, having gained dry footing, were
"followed by the rest of the army; and, charging the
"enemy briskly, put them to flight; but were not able to
"pursue or take the island at that time, *because we had*
"NO CAVALRY; *which was the only thing wanting to com-*
"*pleat* CÆSAR's *wonted success.*

"The

"The enemy being defeated; so soon as they had escaped beyond the reach of danger, sent ambassadors to Cæsar, to desire a peace, promising to deliver hostages for their entire submission; and, with these ambassadors, came Comius of Arras, whom Cæsar had sent into Britain, where he was imprisoned, so soon as he landed with his general's commands, but set at liberty again after the battle."

"They endeavoured to excuse what they had done, by laying the blame upon the mob, and entreating him to forgive a fault of ignorance, but not of malice. Cæsar at first reprimanded them for their breach of faith; that after they had voluntarily sent ambassadors to him into Gaul, to desire a peace, and delivered hostages of their own accord, they should, without any reason, make war upon him!—He imputed it, he said, to their ignorance, and forgave them;—then demanded hostages for their future carriage, part whereof they delivered immediately; and they promised to return, in a few days after, with the rest, who lived at some distance. In the mean time, having disbanded their men, and dispersed them into their several counties, the princes, from all parts, came to deliver up themselves and their estates to Cæsar's disposal."

Affairs did not long remain in this amicable situation, for a violent storm dispersed the eighteen transports, appointed to bring the Roman cavalry, and did considerable damage to Cæsar's fleet in the Downs. The first were forced back again to Gaul, and the latter rendered totally unfit for service. The intelligence of these accidents, threw the Roman army into the utmost consternation, and excited the Britons to revolt. The assembly of princes exhorted the people to seize upon this opportunity of regaining their liberty; and, by a total extermination of

their

their enemies, to deter others from the idea of invading their country. And the Druids took care to observe, that as the heavens interested themselves in their favour, it would be impious not to join the elements in their own deliverance.

Cæsar, in the mean time, did all that a great general, and a prudent man could effect, upon such an emergency. He fortified his camp with great precaution, assiduously furnished it with as much corn as could be procured, and industriously repaired the ships that had received the least damage, with the timber of twelve that were the most shattered.

Hostilities, however, soon commenced; for the seventh legion, being sent out to forage, was suddenly surrounded by the Britons, while the men were unsuspicious and unprepared for an attack. The contest was sharp and bloody, and the Romans would have been totally destroyed, had not Cæsar came seasonably to their relief, and, with his whole force, interposed to save them from destruction. Encouraged by this success, and by the difficulties to which they were sensible the Romans were driven, they surrounded Cæsar's camp, and attacked it with great impetuosity; but, after a bloody conflict, were repulsed with considerable loss; when Cæsar thought proper to lay waste the country for several miles round.

This induced them to send a third embassy to Cæsar, again to apologize for their conduct, and sue for peace. Cæsar severely reprimanded the deputies, and then granted their desires; only insisting to have the number of hostages doubled, and sent after him to Gaul, whither he returned with all his troops on the 20th of September. But the Britons were no sooner freed from such disagreeable company, than most of them forgot their promises;

and

and we find that only two princes thought proper to send the hostages stipulated for in the treaty.

Thus ended Cæsar's first expedition to Britain; which, though glossed over by the Roman self-flattering historian, was *inglorious* to their army, and not of the least solid advantage to the state. Cæsar, however, had sufficient address to represent it of such vast importance, that he was decreed a triumph of twenty days upon the occasion.

CÆSAR'S SECOND INVASION.

During the winter, Cæsar made vast preparations for a more successful expedition in the ensuing summer. Every thing at length being ready, he set sail for Portus Itius, now Boulogne, in the beginning of August, with a fleet of upwards of 800 sail, and a formidable force on board. He landed, without opposition, in the same place he had done the preceding summer, the Britons having retired up the country. Cæsar having left ten cohorts and three hundred horse to guard the ships, penetrated the same night twelve miles from the sea, and discovered the Britons near the river Stour, in Kent. An engagement ensued, when the Britons being routed by the Roman *cavalry*, retreated to a fortified wood, " where," says Cæsar, " they were possessed of a post extremely well " fortified, both by art and nature, which had been built, " in all probability, during the times of their own civil " wars; all the passages to it being blocked up by heaps " of trees, cut down for that purpose. They never " ventured out of this place, but in small parties, and
" always

" always hindered the Romans from entering it; but the
" soldiers of the seventh legion having cast themselves
" into a testudo, and thrown up a mount against their
" works, took the place, and drove them from the
" woods."

THE next morning Cæsar divided his army into three parts, in order to pursue the Britons, but was diverted from this design, by receiving the melancholy intelligence that his fleet was almost destroyed by a storm. He immediately repaired to the sea coast, gave orders to repair some of the ships with the wrecks of others, wrote to Gaul for more, and then resolved upon putting into execution one of the most astonishing expedients that ever entered the mind of man, which was no other than drawing up his navy on dry land, and surrounding it with a fortification. This was effected, by incredible labour and indefatigable industry.

CÆSAR then returned to the place where he had last defeated the ennemy, when " he found far greater numbers
" of the Britons assembled, than he left when he went to
" visit the fleet. By general consent, the whole management
" of this war was committed to the care of Cassive-
" launus, whose territories were divided by the River
" Thames from the sea coasts, and extended four-score
" miles into the island; for, though he had formerly made
" war on the rest of his countrymen, yet, upon our arrival,
" they all united, and pitched upon him as the fittest per-
" son to direct them at so important a conjuncture.

THE Britons attacked the Romans in their march, a sharp conflict ensued, and the former were repulsed; but they soon after made an attempt upon the camp, and broke through two of the best cohorts.

CÆSAR,

Cæsar, in relating this affair, is under the necessity of acknowledging, that he had rather the disadvantage. His words are, "This engagement happening in the view of the whole army, every one perceived that the legionary soldiers were not a fit match for such an enemy; because the weight of their armour would not permit them to pursue, nor durst they go too far from their colours, neither could the cavalry encounter them; because *the Britons often pretended a retreat, and, having drawn them from the legions, would forsake their chariots, and fight on foot to great advantage; and, when they were mounted, they were equally fatal to our horse, whether we pursued or fled.* Another disadvantage was, that the enemy never fought in a close battalion, but *in small parties, at a great distance from one another, each of them having their particular part allotted, from whence they received supplies, and the weary were relieved by the fresh.*"

The next day the Britons attacked three legions that were foraging, but were repulsed with considerable loss. Upon this ill success, the auxiliaries forsook Cassivelaunus, who was never after able to bring any formidable force into the field.

Not being able to make head against the Romans, the unfortunate British chief retreated to his own territories, and fortified the Thames, where fordable. The Romans, however, forced a passage at Coway, in Middlesex, and proceeded on their march, when they were met by deputies from the magistrates of the chief city of the Trinobantes, who ignobly offered subjection, and traiterously joined the Romans; at the same time requesting that Mandubratius, one of Cæsar's attendants, whose father was killed by Cassivelaunus, might be permitted to rule them. Cæsar assented, but at the same time demanded forty hostages, and provisions for his whole army.

C These

These conditions were complied with; and the defection of those people not only weakened the common cause, but induced several other states to follow their example. Among those who joined Cæsar, some were base enough to let him know what strength Cassivellaunus had still remaining, and where he had retreated to. Upon this information, Cæsar immediately proceeded to the city of Verulam, now St. Alban's, and besieged that unfortunate chief in his capital. The place was tolerably well fortified with woods and morasses; but the Romans took it by storm, and put a prodigious number of the unhappy Britons to the sword. Cassivellaunus, however, escaped; and, as his last resource, persuaded four petty kings of Kent, viz. Cingetorix, Carvilius, Taximagulas, and Segonax, to attack the Roman camp, where the ships were secured, and try to destroy the navy. The project was put in execution, but failed of success; for the Britons were defeated, and Cingetorix taken prisoner. This ill success, the desolation of his country, and the revolt of his allies, induced Cassivellaunus at length to sue for peace.

His request was granted immediately by Cæsar, who pretended to have a great respect for Cassivellaunus, on account of his personal courage; but the real reason of his granting him conditions tolerably favourable, was his desire to return to Gaul, where the public affairs rendered his immediate presence necessary. Previous to his departure, he imposed a yearly tribute upon the Britons; included his ally, Mandubratius, in the treaty; and tried to secure the allegiance of the different kingdoms, by taking with him a great number of hostages.

Thus concludes Cæsar's second invasion, wherein Tacitus observes, he had rather *shewn* Britain to the Romans, than *given them possession of it*. When he returned to Rome, the British captives, from their remarkable attire, and peculiarity

of

of manners, afforded matter of admiration to the people; and Cæsar offered a breast-plate, embroidered with pearls, found in Britain, to Venus, as a trophy of the spoils of the ocean.

The subjugation of a great part of Britain, was the very last triumph of the Romans, who had conquered so many nations in Europe, Asia, and Africa, for the purpose of extending their territories. Cæsar himself placed it among the greatest of his achievments, boasting that he had discovered and penetrated into a new world.

If this great general, in writing his history, had been accused of turning every thing to his own advantage, never does he seem to lay under stronger suspicions of doing so than in this affair. We cannot read the particulars of his two invasions, without being sensible there is something wanting; and that which is passed over in silence, was not at all to his honour.

He sets out from Gaul, as Dion Cassius assures us, with an intent to conquer and reduce the whole island to a Roman province. He, every where, gets the better of the Britons. He passes the Thames, in spite of all obstacles. Cassivellaunus finding he could not oppose him, dismisses his troops. Cæsar becomes master of his capital; and the Britons submit and sue for peace. After this, he is contented with imposing a light tribute on Cassivellaunus; and, without fortifying any one place, or leaving any troops in the island, he drops his first design, satisfied with restoring Mandubratius; as if the war had been undertaken solely on his account. Does not this make it very suspicious, that he was *forced* to accede to those terms? Lucan, though no friend to him, would not, without some grounds, have accused him as he did, " *of turning his back to the Britons.*" Dion tells us, that in an action, the Britons entirely routed the Roman infantry,

fantry, but were afterwards put into disorder by the cavalry. Horace and Tibullus infinuate, in feveral places of their works, *that the Britons were not looked upon as conquered by the Romans.*

From all this it is evident, that the reputation Cæsar acquired by these two invasions, was not near so great as is represented in his Commentaries.

AUGUSTUS'S INTENDED INVASION.

The Emperor Agustus, Cæsar's immediate successor, greatly neglected this island for several years; at length he determined to invade Britain, but was diverted from his purpose by a revolt in Panonia. About seven years afterwards, he renewed his design; but the distracted state of Gaul, and the arrival of some ambassadors from Britain, to sue for a peace, caused him a second time to change his resolution. The ensuing year he again reassumed his intention, and was again disappointed by commotions in other parts. Thus all his plans of invading Britain, proved abortive. Tiberius succeeded Augustus, and, like his predecessor, paid but little regard to Britain.

CALIGULA'S THREATENED INVASION.

On the death of Tiberius, the empire devolved to Caligula, a most capricious, inconsistent, and cruel tyrant. In his reign, Adminius, the son of Cunobelin, a British king, raised an unnatural rebellion against his father; but, not succeeding

[13]

ceeding according to his wish, he fled to Caligula, who, being of a base disposition himself, received the traitor with open arms. The treacherous Briton, finding the encouragement given to his crimes, and perceiving the weakness of the emperor, persuaded him to invade not only his father's dominions, but those of all the other British princes; representing, that the conquest would be very important from the riches it would bring; extremely glorious from its importance, and by no means difficult, from the terrors of his name; for the Britons, said he, will throw down their arms, the moment they hear you are coming in person against them.

These arguments exactly suited the avarice, pride, and cowardice of the emperor; who thought that an opportunity to gain wealth and fame, without danger, was not to be neglected. He accordingly drew together an army of *two hundred thousand* men, to invade Britain, and proceeded to the coast of Belgic Gaul. He was here informed, to his great surprize, that the Britons were under arms on the opposite shore, with a determined resolution to oppose his intended descent. This, at first, he could hardly believe. Being, however, at length convinced that his name was not so terrible as he imagined, his fears induced him to desist; for he resolved not to engage in any enterprize, attended with the least personal danger. But, that it should not be said he was afraid to *see* his enemies, he embarked on board a galley, sailed within a league of the British coast, took *a peep* at the Britons, whose formidable appearance he did not at all like; and then hasted back, with as much ostentation, as if he had achieved some great action.

To make himself more ridiculous, he ordered the army to be drawn up in battle array, as soon as he landed; and, having made a curious harangue to all the soldiers, to their utter astonishment, gave directions that they should disperse themselves about the sea coast, to gather up all the

shells

shells they could find! The troops naturally thought the emperor's head was turned, but, at the same time, obeyed.

A PRODIGIOUS quantity of shells being collected, Caligula commanded that they should be carefully packed up; and, to compleat the farce, sent them with the most pompous parade to Rome, as the spoils of the British ocean; demanding, at the same time, that the senate should decree him a triumph, for the important services he had done the empire. Absurd as this request may appear, the senate was civil enough to comply with it; and put themselves to immense expence, to render the emperor magnificently ridiculous in the face of the whole world.

CLAUDIUS'S INVASION.

THUS, from the continual failure of intended invasions, the Britons remained unassailed by the Romans, from Julius Cæsar till the reign of Claudius; and *then rather fell victims to their own intestine broils, than to the power of that empire.*— *Jealousy did what their enemies' sword could not effect; and while some kings had the virtue to oppose the Romans, others joined them, and were solicitors for their own destruction.* BERIC, a discontented British prince, was the chief enemy to his own country, and the principal person who persuaded the emperor to undertake the expedition.

PLAUTIUS, the prætor, was placed at the head of the army, and ordered to pass into Britain. But the troops mutinied, and declared, "They would not make war out " of the compass of the world;" for the common people
thought,

thought, that all places, beyond the ocean, were out of the limits of the world to which they belonged. At length, threats, presents, and promises, prevailed; harmony was restored; and the troops reconciled to the expedition. Plautius took advantage of this favourable disposition, and embarked his whole force, at three ports, that the failure of one embarkation might not prevent the success of the enterprize. They were, however, all driven back, by contrary winds, and much disheartened. But the appearance of an *aurora borealis*, recalled their spirits; for the Romans, imagining this meteor to be a happy omen, again set sail, and landed in Britain, without opposition. Their not meeting with the resistance they expected, was owing to the Britons having been informed, by some merchants, that the Roman troops had mutinied, and the invasion was laid aside. This fatal intelligence soothed them into security, and occasioned them to disband their forces, when there was more necessity than ever to employ them.

PLAUTIUS penetrated as far as Oxfordshire, without any opposition, except being a little harrassed by small skirmishing parties. He now advanced toward the principal forces that the Britons had been able to collect, which were very impolitically divided into two bodies, the one commanded by Caractacus, and the other by Togodumnus, his brother. Plautius attacked them seperately, and defeated both parties. This double misfortune threw the Britons into great consternation; and at the same time determined Plautius to make every advantage of his success; leaving a sufficient body of troops to secure the country already conquered, he proceeded to the Isis. As this river was not fordable, they imagined it would have stopped the career of the Romans. Their mistake was, however, soon evident; for Plautius ordered the German auxiliaries to plunge into the stream, and swim over, which they easily effected, though encumbered by their armour; for these people were trained fror

their

their youth, to swim across deep and rapid streams, while incommoded with heavy weights. The Germans no sooner gained the opposite shore, than, according to the order of their general, they aimed their arrows and darts at the horses of the enemy; and, by the slaughter of those animals, rendered the chariots useless.

The Romans, animated by the example of the Germans, soon crossed the river to their support; when the Britons, unequal to the conflict, fled. The next day, however, they recovered their spirits, and attacked the Romans with such impetuosity, that a victory would have been the consequence, had not Sideus Geta, after having been taken prisoner, freed himself, and those who were with him, and charged the Britons in the rear. This unexpected attack, threw them into great consternation, and a rout ensued. Geta was deemed the cause of the victory, and a triumph was afterwards decreed him upon that account, though he had never passed the Consular dignity.

The Britons then marched expeditiously along the banks of the Thames, and forded it at places with which they were well acquainted; while the Romans, who followed them, were frequently bemired in bogs and marshes. At length discovering a ford, the latter passed over, and again defeated the former; when many Britons, among whom was Prince Togodumnus, were slain.

Plautius found that his own army was considerably diminished, by these repeated engagements; and that the Britons, not discouraged by their ill successes, were still determined to struggle for their liberties. Doubtful of his own security, he sent to the continent for reinforcements, and strongly solicited the emperor to come in person, in order to compleat the conquest.

Claudius

Claudius accordingly landed in Britain in the month of August, A. D. 43, with a powerful army, and immediately marched to join Plautius, whose troops were encamped on the south side of the Thames. The forces, by their junction, formed a more considerable army than the Romans had ever before brought into the island. Claudius took the sole command upon himself, marched expeditiously up to the Britons, and before they had time to reflect, brought them to a general engagement, in which they received a total overthrow.

This last fatal defeat, and the powerful army of the Romans, quite dispirited the Britons, who thought more of making their peace, than retrieving their affairs; and determined to court the confidence, instead of opposing the progress of the conqueror. They accordingly, in general, threw down their arms; and ambassadors from the different princes, flocked daily to the Roman camp, to make their submission. It is therefore, at this period, that we ought to date the general reduction of the Britons, by the Romans; for the previous invasions tended rather to disturb than subjugate the country. Claudius then took Camulodunum, now Malden, in Essex, which he made a military colony. A great part of the country was reduced to a Roman province; and, having conciliated the affections of the Britons, by his moderation, he returned to the continent.

The Romans having now secured a footing in the island, all their future efforts to subdue it completely, may be rather termed expeditions than invasions. But, during the whole period of their dominion in this country, they never entirely subjugated it to their yoke. For the northern parts of it still remained free. As for the incursions of Agricola and Severus, they were rather temporary inroads, than decisive conquests. All the high-spirited Britons,

Britons, who disdained yielding to the Roman sway, fled thither, and preserved their liberty in the mountains of the north.

CHAP. II.

INVASIONS OF THE SAXONS.

THE Roman Empire, in the reigns of Arcadius and Honorius, was torne to pieces within, by intestine quarrels; and was powerfully attacked without, by barbarous nations, that made horrible ravages upon the frontiers. The period was now arrived, when that enormous fabric, which had diffused slavery and oppression, together with civility and peace, over so considerable a part of the globe, was approaching towards its final dissolution, by an inundation of barbarians from the north; who not only over-run the exterior provinces, but threatened the destruction of the central provinces, and even Rome itself.

In this dilemma, the emperors, *instead of arming the people in their own defence,* recalled all the distant legions. All the Roman troops, in Britain, were consequently carried over to the protection of Gaul and Italy.

The Britons, though secured by the sea, against the invasion of the greatest tribes of barbarians, found enemies on its frontiers, who took advantage of its present defenceless situation. For, however much the Romans had polished them by letters, by science, and by manners, they were, at the same time, rendered so dispirited and submissive, by being disarmed as well as enslaved, that they had lost all desire, and even idea, of their former liberty and independence.

The Picts and Scots, who dwelt in the northern parts of the island, seized upon this favourable opportunity of the absence of the Roman troops, to make incursions upon their peaceable and effeminate neighbours. Besides the temporary depredations which they committed, these combined nations threatened the whole south with subjection; or, what the inhabitants more dreaded, with plunder and devastation. The Britons, accustomed to have recourse to the Roman Emperors for defence, as well as government, made supplications to Rome, and one legion was sent over for their protection. This small force was an over-match for the barbarous invaders, who were routed in every engagement; and, having chaced them into their ancient limits, returned in triumph, to the defence of the southern provinces of the empire.

The retreat of the Romans, however, only served to bring on a new invasion of the enemy. Again the Britons made an application to Rome, and again obtained the assistance of a legion, which proved effectual for their relief. But the Romans, reduced to extremities at home, informed the Britons that they must no longer look to them for succour; *and exhorted them to* ARM *in their own defence.* They besides urged, *that, as they were now their own masters, it became them to* PROTECT, *by their* VALOUR, *that* INDEPENDENCE *which their ancient Lords had conferred upon them.* After having assisted them in fortifying the frontiers, they bade a final adieu to Britain, having been

masters

masters of the more considerable part of it during the course of near four centuries.

WHAT an abject state were the Britons then thrown into, from effeminacy and want of discipline! They had not even the spirit to ARM *themselves!* For, regarding this *present* of LIBERTY as *fatal*, they were in no condition to put in practice the prudent counsel given them by the Romans, " To ARM *in their own* DEFENCE !" Unaccustomed, both to the perils of war, and to the cares of civil government, they found themselves incapable of forming or executing any measures for resisting the incursions of their barbarous neighbours.

THE Picts and Scots, finding that the Romans had now totally abandoned Britain, regarded the whole as their prey; and carried, every where, devastation and ruin. They exerted, to their utmost, their native ferocity; which was by no means mitigated, by the hopeless condition and submissive behaviour of the wretched inhabitants.

NOTWITHSTANDING the resolution of the Romans, to abandon them for ever, the Britons had recourse, a third time, to their protection. They wrote, upon this occasion, such a degrading letter to Ætius, the Roman general, then in Gaul, as cannot be perused without indignation and contempt. The tenor of this dastardly epistle was:

" THE GROANS OF THE BRITONS!

" *We know not which way to turn us. The Barbarians*
" *drive us to the sea; the sea drives us back to the Barbarians;*
" *and we have only the hard choice left us, either to be butch-*
" *ered by the sword, or swallowed up by the waves!*"

IT is almost incredible to think, that such a numerous people as the Britons, could be so far enfeebled by the
Romans,

Romans, as not to be able to defend themselves against such a contemptible enemy; for contemptible must that enemy be, when a Roman legion, consisting of less than 4000 men, could defeat and expel them, however fierce and brave those two invading nations have been represented to posterity. The only reason that can be assigned for such unaccountable imbecility, is, that the Romans, every year, drained their British provinces of all the youths fit to bear arms, and sent them to recruit their armies on the continent; so that between the enfeebling of the minds of the Britons, and the depriving them of all the vigorous aid of the flower of their youth, by the policy of their Roman masters, they may be said to have been a nation without men, as well as a people without courage. The Romans cherished those shoots which they transplanted; they benumbed those, which they permitted to remain.

When we reflect, that their whole military establishment here, was not 20,000 foot, and 2000 cavalry, it seems wonderful that their utmost skill and rigour was able, for near four centuries, to keep such a populous nation in subjection, as the Britons. This historical lesson, therefore, shews us the absolute necessity of keeping up the martial spirit of the British empire, that, upon every urgent occasion of defence, like the present, we may be " *A powerful armed nation,*" as well as " *A great commercial State.*"--To return:

Ætius, having to contend with Attila, who had entered Gaul with an immense army, consisting of no less than 800,000 men, sent the Britons for answer, that the affairs of the empire would by no means permit him to comply with their request. The abject, wretched Britons, were thunder-struck at this, and reduced to despair. After several severe conflicts, and being on the precipice of ruin,

ruin, their provincial kings agreed to chuse a supreme monarch, from among themselves, to guide them in this dreadful moment. Their choice fell on Vortigern, king of the western counties of Devonshire and Cornwall. Instead of following the advice of the Romans, *by* ARMING *and* DISCIPLINING *themselves*, he fatally advised them to call in the aid of the *Saxons*.

THAT race of men had been, for some time, regarded as one of the most warlike tribes of the fierce Germans, and had become the terror of the neighbouring nations. They had taken possession of all the sea coast from the mouth of the Rhine to Jutland; whence they had long infested, by their piracies, all the eastern and southern parts of Britain, and the northern parts of Gaul. The Romans, in order to oppose their inroads, had established an officer, whom they called Count of the Saxon shore; and, as the naval arts can flourish among a civilized people alone, they seem to have been more successful in repelling the Saxons, than any other of the barbarians by whom they were invaded. The dissolution of the Roman power invited them to renew their inroads; and it was an acceptable circumstance, that the ambassadors of the Britons appeared among them, and prompted them to undertake an enterprize to which they were of themselves sufficiently inclined. The name of Saxons they received from the Gothic word *Seax*, which implies a short, crooked, or hooked sword, that they wore as their principal weapon, and for the dextrous use of which they were much celebrated.

THEY gladly accepted this invitation of the Britons, and an aid of 9000 men was granted them, on condition that the Saxons were put in possession of the Isle of Thanet, and their troops allowed a certain pay. They did not think proper, however, to send over at once the stipulated number of troops, to a country of which they were but imperfectly acquainted.

quainted. About 1500, who were selected by lot, set sail, under the command of Hengist and Horsa, sons of the Saxon general. They were carried to Thanet, in three keyles or large transport boats, when they immediately marched to the defence of the Britons, by attacking the Picts and Scots. They who were advanced as far as Stamford in Lincolnshire, were entirely routed by the Saxons, and soon driven back to their own barren regions with great loss.

But those brave auxiliaries in their various marches through the country, beholding its beauty, verdure and fertility, were desirous of possessing it themselves. Perceiving the Britons enervated by luxury, sunk in vice, and lost to those noble sentiments of freedom, which can inspire true courage, their ambition was awakened to the idea of ruling those they came to defend, and enslaving a people they had been employed to protect.

The youthful Saxon commander, sent home intelligence of the richness of Britain; and represented, *as certain, the subjection of a people so* LONG DISUSED TO ARMS, DISUNITED *among themselves,* DESTITUTE *of all national* ATTACHMENT, *and lost to every sense of the blessings acquired by their recent* LIBERTY, granted them by the Romans. They were immediately reinforced with 5000 men, consisting of Saxons, Jutes, and Angles, who came over in seventeen vessels. The Britons now began to entertain apprehensions of their allies, whose numbers they found continually augmenting, but thought of no remedy, except a passive submission and connivance. This weak expedient failed them. The Saxons sought a quarrel, by complaining that their subsidies were ill paid, and their provisions withdrawn. And, immediately taking off the mask, they formed an alliance with the Picts and Scots, and proceeded to open hostility against the Britons.

Mass

Many battles were fought between them, which generally terminated in favour of the Saxons. Hengist, continually reinforced by fresh numbers of auxiliary invaders, from Germany, carried devastation into the most remote corners of Britain; and being chiefly anxious to spread the terror of his arms; he spared neither sex, nor age, nor condition, wherever he marched with his victorious forces. The private and public edifices of the Britons, were reduced to ashes: The priests were slaughtered on the altars by those idolatrous ravagers: The bishops and nobility shared the fate of the vulgar: The people, flying to the mountains and deserts, were intercepted, and butchered in heaps: Some were glad to accept of life, and servitude under the victors: Others, deserting their native country, took shelter in the province of Armorica; where being charitably received by a people of the same language and manners, they settled in a great number, and gave the country the name of Brittany.

Thus, after a violent contest of near 150 years, the Heptarchy, or seven Saxon kingdoms, was established in Britain; and, in that time, by various invasions and expulsions, the whole southern part of the island, except Wales and Cornwall, had totally changed its inhabitants, language, customs, and political institutions. The Britons, under the Roman dominion, had made such advances towards arts and civil manners, that they had built twenty-eight considerable cities, within their province, besides a great number of villages and country seats. But the fierce Saxons threw every thing back into ancient barbarity; and those few natives, who were not either massacred or expelled their habitations, were reduced to the most abject slavery.

The first Saxon invaders, from Germany, instead of excluding other adventurers, who must share with them the spoils of the ancient inhabitants, were obliged to solicit

fresh

fresh supplies from their own country; and a total extermination of the Britons, became the sole expedient for providing a settlement and subsistence to the new planters.

To mention all the different swarms of auxiliary invaders, that came over here, during the wars between the Saxons and the Britons, is not altogether practicable, nor indeed is it necessary. It will be sufficient to recount the chief hordes of them who arrived at different periods, that the reader may have some idea of the successive invading force, which the Britons had to combat.

HENGIST, finding that the 6500 men were by no means competent to the task of conquest and extirpation, sent for a fleet of forty ships, full of Saxon forces, under the command of his brother, Octa. They plundered the Orcades, drove the Picts northward, and at first settled on the north side of the Tine, eastwards; but soon advanced towards the south, and chaced the Britons beyond the Humber. With this reinforcement, acting in a distant part of the island, he had little to fear from the Britons; although he still continued to send for, and obtain, more supplies of men, for his own army, on pretence of wanting recruits.

AFTERWARDS, Hengist sent for Ella, a Saxon general, from Germany, promising him a part of the island. Ella, glad of the news, soon arrived in Britain, and landed his troops at Whitering, in Sussex, but not without opposition. The inhabitants of the country, disputing his landing, he became not master of the shore, till after a long battle. At length, he drove the Britons far up the country; the victors settled along the southern coast, and were called South Saxons, and their country Sussex.

CERDICK, another Saxon general, arrived at Yarmouth, in Norfolk, with five ships, full of troops; and defeated the

the Britons, who were waiting to dispute his landing. He founded the kingdom of Wessex, or that of the West Saxons.

PORTA, another Saxon general, arrived at Portland, so called from him, with a new reinforcement of Saxons, from Germany.

STUFF and Withgar, the nephews of Cerdick, arrived with a great force, from Germany, to assist their uncle.

MULTITUDES of Angles, under the conduct of twelve chiefs, all of equal authority, landed on the eastern coast of Britain; and, continually gaining ground towards the west, they compelled, at length, the Britons to abandon the country along the eastern shore. Thus situated, the Angles had an opportunity of sending, from time to time, for fresh colonies from Germany; and founded, by this means, the kingdom of the East Angles.

CERDICK, after he was king, acquainted all his countrymen, who chose to settle in his dominions, that they should meet with great encouragement, if they would join him. Above 800 vessels, soon after this invitation, arrived in his ports, on board of which were a vast number of Saxons and Jutes, with their families.

IDA, an Angle, embarked a considerable number of his own countrymen, in forty vessels, and landed at Flamborough, in Yorkshire, then in possession of the Northumbrian Saxons, who received them as friends; and he was afterwards made king of Northumberland.

CRIDA, another leader of the Angles, sailed from Germany, with a large fleet, and a greater number of people than had ever arrived, at one time, from Germany. They landed

landed in East Anglia, and, after marching towards the middle of the island, drove the Britons across the Severn into Wales; and founded the kingdom of the Mercians, or Middle Angles, the largest and most considerable of all the Saxon sovereignties.

Thus have we given a brief view of the various great bodies of auxiliary invaders, that joined the Saxons in their conquest of the best parts of Britain. Their numbers, altogether, must be very great, when it is considered that almost each colony established a seperate kingdom; while the Britons never received any foreign aid, but once from Brittany, and once from Scotland, neither of which proved of any lasting utility.

But the *dissentions* of the Britons, as well as their want of military discipline and spirit, was a principal cause of their destruction. Had they been *more united, and trusted more to their own exertions*, they would have defended themselves better against the first Saxon allies, when they became invaders; and, by that means, have discouraged others from attempting to invade the island.

When we reflect on the weakness and want of spirit of the Britons, at the arrival of Hengist, we are surprised at their being able to make any defence at all, against the Saxon power. But a long war teaches the most unwarlike nations the use of arms, and very frequently puts them in a condition to repair, in the end, those losses which they sustained in the beginning. Had the Saxons, at first, invaded Britain, with a numerous army, they would have most probably conquered it in a very short period. But they spun out the war, by sending over a small number of forces only at once, and thereby revived an art which the Romans had almost totally destroyed.

Although

Although the Britons were rendered so abject by the Roman policy, that a few thousands of their troops, nay 1500 Saxons, were able to repel their ferocious enemies, the Picts and Scots, which they could not accomplish, upon their old masters leaving the island; yet it is well known that their succeeding dreadful conflicts restored their ancient valour, and taught them the most expert discipline. How else could they have withstood the whole power of the Saxons, Jutes, and Angles, for near a century and a half, and with such resolute bravery, that if fresh numbers of invaders, from the continent, had not poured continually in upon them, there is every probability of their having remained victorious!

We may draw, however, some wise instruction from the misfortunes of the Britons. *When we can afford* RECIPROCAL *aid to our allies, the forming of treaties is the political cement of society. But, if we neglect to* ARM OURSELVES, *on every fit occasion, and to infuse* SPIRIT *and* DISCIPLINE *among our fellow subjects*, our allies might soon become our masters, and we should sink into insignificance, poverty, slavery, and contempt.

CHAP. III.

INVASIONS OF THE DANES.

THE Saxon princes preserved an union of counsels and interests, so long as the contest was maintained with the natives; but, after the Britons were shut up in the steril countries of Cornwall and Wales, and gave no farther disturbance to the conquerors, the band of alliance was, in a great measure, dissolved among the princes of the Heptarchy. Dissentions and wars, therefore, became unavoidable.

THE Danes, during these commotions, made several petty invasions on Britain, before their naval power became so alarming to the Anglo Saxons. The situation of their country, and the great plenty of all materials necessary for building and equipping a fleet, soon made them very strong at sea. For above 300 years, the Danish pirates were, in a manner, lords of the ocean. Though they were sometimes repulsed and defeated by the Angles, or English, they generally obtained their end, of committing spoil upon the country, and carrying off their booty.

THEY avoided coming to a general engagement, which was not suited to their plan of operation. Their vessels were small, and ran easily up the creeks and rivers; where they drew them ashore, and, having formed an entrenchment

ment round them, which they guarded with part of their number, the remainder scattered themselves every where, and, carrying off the inhabitants, the cattle, and goods, they hastened to their ships, and quickly disappeared.

If the military force of the country were assembled, for there was no time for troops to march from a distance, the Danes either were able to repulse them, and to continue their ravages with impunity, or they betook themselves to their vessels; and, setting sail, suddenly invaded some distant quarter, which was not prepared for their reception. Every part of England was, at length, held in continual alarm; and the inhabitants of one country durst not give assistance to those of another, lest their own families and property should, in the mean time, be exposed, by their absence, to the fury of these barbarous ravagers.

The first of their invasions, was in the year 787, when they landed on the south west coast of England, in the kingdom of Wessex. A small body of them landed there, with a view of learning the state of the country; and, when the magistrate of the place questioned them concerning their enterprize, and summoned them to appear before the king, and account for their intentions, they killed him; and, flying to their ships, escaped into their own country.

In about seven years after, they made a more formidable invasion. They landed in Northumberland, and burnt Lindisfarne monastery. Allured by the booty they had taken, in their first expedition, they returned in the following year, and pillaged Tinmouth monastery. Ethelrid, the reigning king of Northumberland, by the assistance of Offa, king of Mercia, prevented them from carrying their ravages any farther, and drove them to their ships. Nearly the whole of them perished on the coast, in a violent storm.

THEIR

Their petty incursions now became almost annual; and they were dreaded, not only throughout all this island, but also along the coast of several other European kingdoms; as they every where committed great ravages. The vast booty they obtained, tempted the richest and most powerful of their countrymen to embark for plunder. They invaded the provinces of France, and were called there, Normans, men from the north. In England, they were generally stiled Danes, or Goths.

The Heptarchy was hardly dissolved, and England formed into one kingdom, under the dominion of Egbert, when the Danes again invaded England; they landed in the isle of Shepey, in Kent, and, having pillaged it, escaped with impunity.

Next year they attempted another invasion, and landed at Charmouth, in Dorsetshire. Their fleet consisted of thirty-five sail. In their usual manner, they immediately pillaged the country. Though Egbert attacked them with great spirit, his army was entirely routed, after a long and stubborn engagement. The Danes pressed so hard on him, in his retreat, that he was indebted for his life to the darkness of the night. Egbert, who had always been victorious till then, was extremely mortified at being worsted, which made him adopt more vigorous measures for his defence, against these new invaders. The Danes, in the mean time, having no designs to make conquests, returned to their ships, after plundering all the surrounding country.

Another band of Danish invaders, having been informed by their spies, that the Cornish Britons were desirous of throwing off the English yoke, landed in Cornwall, where they were received with great joy. After being reinforced with some British troops, they marched, in order to give battle to Egbert. Each party were endeavouring to rufh upon action, by furprize, and confequently both were prepared. The difcomfiture of Egbert having made him more wary, he kept his army in readinefs to march, upon the firft notice of their arrival. Therefore, upon being informed, that they were landed in the weft, he went thither at the head of all his troops, with great expedition, and obtained a fignal victory over them, near Hengftor Hill, in Cornwall, which wiped out the difgrace of his former defeat.

The Danes foon afterwards invaded England, in the beginning of the reign of Ethelwulph, Egbert's only fon. They appeared off Southampton. After hovering about for fome time, they landed and ravaged the flat country. Ethelwulph fent Wulfred, his general, againft them, who foon drove them back to their fhips. But the army had hardly returned, when fome more Danes landed at Portland, and fet about plundering and ravaging the country. Earl Ethelhelm, who now commanded the Englifh forces, was fhamefully beaten, and put to flight.

Herbert, another commander, was not only vanquifhed, but flain. The Danes, in confequence of thefe two victories, over-run feveral counties; particularly Kent and Middlefex. Canterbury, Rochefter, and London, were terribly harraffed; and the enemy, after committing great cruelties, returned to their fhips.

The following year, another body of Danes landed on the coaft of Dorfetfhire. Their fleet confifted of thirty-five fail. Ethelwulph led his troops in perfon. againft the enemy. An action took place, at Charmouth, wherein the Englifh where completely defeated; and the Danes, after plundering the country, the only aim at firft of all thefe expeditions, fet fail for Denmark.

In

In the year 845, the Danes, landing in Somersetshire, were defeated near the river Parret, and the English obtained such a decisive victory, as deterred them, for some years, from all invasion of the southern coasts of England.

But the troubles and dissensions, in the kingdom of Northumberland, gave the Danes frequent opportunities of plundering that coast. Whenever they arrived, they were sure to be joined by the EX-PARTY. *The minor faction made no scruple to join with the common enemy, in order to gain the ascendancy: and assisted in the destruction of their country, for the sake of enjoying authority.*

The Danes, in 851, invaded the southern coast, and committed the most horrid cruelties. On their return to their ships, however, being laden and encumbered with their booty, they were attacked by the English commander, at Westbury, in Dorsetshire, and entirely defeated. King Athelstan, soon after, equipping out a fleet, engaged the Danes off Sandwich, and captured nine of their ships; but all his skill and force could not prevent them from wintering in the isle of Shepey. This was the first time they ventured to seize territory here, as well as plunder.

In the spring, a strong reinforcement of their countrymen arriving, in 350 ships, they advanced from the isle of Thanet, where they had stationed themselves; burnt the cities of London and Canterbury, marched into the heart of Surry, and laid every place waste around them. Ethelwulf, impelled by the urgency of the danger, marched against them, at the head of the West Saxons; and, carrying with him his second son, Ethelbald, gave them battle at Okely, and gained a bloody victory over them. They made so terrible a slaughter of the Danes, that very few escaped. This advantage proved but a short respite to the English.

F

The

The Danes still possessed the isle of Thanet, and, being attacked by the governors of Kent and Surry, though defeated in the beginning of the action, they finally repulsed the assailants, and killed both the governors. After this, they removed to the isle of Shepey, where they took up their winter quarters, that they might farther extend their devastation and ravages.

All orders of men were now involved in this new calamity of Danish invasion; and the priests and monks, who had been commonly spared in the domestic quarrels of the Heptarchy, were the chief objects on which the Danish idolators exercised their rage and animosity. Every season of the year was dangerous; and the absence of the enemy was no reason why any man could esteem himself a moment in safety.

They invaded the south coast, in 860, penetrated as far as Winchester, and reduced that city to ashes, but were afterwards beat back to their ships.

They landed about two years after, in the isle of Thanet, where they wintered, in order to be ready to make incursions in the spring. Ethelbert, dreading their power, offered them a sum of money to retire, which they promised to do; but, on receiving it, they rushed into Kent, and destroyed all with fire and sword. Ethelbert levied an army to intercept them in their retreat, and prevent them from carrying off their booty. But the dread of these preparations made them embark so suddenly, that he could not prevent it.

In the year 866, the Danes began a very formidable invasion of England. Prompted by there own avarice, *and invited by a treacherous English nobleman,* named Bruern Brocard, they landed in East Anglia; the inhabitants of which, more anxious for their present safety, than for the

common

common interest of England, entered into a separate treaty with them, and furnished them with horses, which enabled them to make an irruption by land, into the kingdom of Northumberland. They besieged the city of York, and defeated the tributary princes of Northumberland. Encouraged by these successes, and by the superiority which they had acquired in arms, they now ventured to leave the sea coast, and, penetrating into Mercia, they took up their winter quarters at Nottingham, where they threatened the kingdom with a final subjection.

This so terrified Edmund, that he applied to Ethelred for succour; and that monarch, with his brother Alfred, conducting a great army to Nottingham, obliged the enemy to dislodge, and to retreat to Northumberland. Their restless disposition, and avidity for plunder, allowed them not to remain long in those quarters. They broke into East Anglia, the very country that basely supplied them with horses, and entered into treaty with them; they defeated and took prisoner its prince, and afterwards murdered him in cold blood, by tying him to a tree, and shooting at him, as at a butt, with arrows. Besides, committing the most barbarous ravages on the people, particularly on the monasteries, they gave the East Angles cause to regret the temporary relief which they had obtained, by assisting the common enemy.

Among other cruelties they committed, at this time, was that on the nuns of Coldingham. The Abbess, to prevent herself and the nuns of the abbey from Danish violation, persuaded them to cut off their noses and upper lips; and by her own example, induced them to perform the dreadful operation. The Danes, beholding their shocking appearance, were so exasperated as to set the monastery on fire, when all those virtuous ladies perished together in the flames.

Having subdued East Anglia, the Danes next made a descent in Wessex, and penetrated as far as Reading, in Berkshire, by their incursions. The Mercians, desirous of shaking off their dependance on King Ethelred, refused to join him with their forces: and that prince, attended by Alfred, was obliged to march against the enemy, with the West Saxons alone, his hereditary subjects. The Danes were defeated on Ashdown, principally through the intrepidity of young Alfred. Besides a great number of soldiers, the Danes lost five Earls and a King.

Another battle was fought, about a fortnight after, in which the English had rather the disadvantage, in the beginning of the day. Alfred advancing with one division of his army, was surrounded by the enemy on disadvantageous ground; and Ethelred, who was at that time hearing mass, refused to march to his assistance, till prayers should be finished. But as he afterwards obtained the victory, this success, not the danger of Alfred, was ascribed by the monks to the piety of that monarch. This battle did not terminate the war; another battle was, a little after, fought at Basing, where the Danes were very successful; and, being reinforced by a new army from their own country, they became every day more terrible to the English.

INVASIONS IN ALFRED THE GREAT'S REIGN.

Alfred had scarcely ascended the throne, when he was obliged to take the field, in order to oppose the Danes, who had seized Wilton, and were exercising their usual ravages on the countries around. He marched against
them

them with the few troops which he could assemble on a sudden; and giving them battle, gained at first an advantage; but, by his pursuing the victory too far, the superiority of the enemy's numbers prevailed, and recovered them the day. Their loss, however, in the action, was so considerable, that, fearing Alfred would receive daily reinforcement from his subjects, they stipulated for a safe retreat, and promised to depart the kingdom.

For that purpose they were conducted to London, and allowed to take up winter quarters there; but, careless of their engagements, they immediately set themselves to the committing of spoil on the neighbouring country. Burrhed, king of Mercia, in whose territories London was situated, made a new stipulation with them; and engaged them, by presents of money, to remove to Lindsey, in Lincolnshire, a country which they had already reduced to ruin and desolation.

Finding no object in that place, either for rapine or violence, they suddenly turned back upon Mercia, in a quarter where they expected to find it, without defence; and, fixing their station at Repton, in Derbyshire, they laid the whole country desolate with fire and sword. Burrhed, despairing of success against an enemy whom no force could resist, and no treaties bind, abandoned his kingdom; and, flying to Rome, took shelter in a cloister. He was brother-in-law to Alfred, and the last who bore the title of king, in Mercia, or the Middle Counties.

The West Saxons were now the only remaining power in England; and though supported by the vigour and abilities of Alfred, they were unable to sustain the efforts of those ravagers; who, from all quarters, invaded them. A new swarm of Danes came over this year, under three princes, Guthrum, Oscital, and Amund; and having
first

first joined their countrymen, at Repton, they found the necessity of separating, in order to provide for their subsistence.

Part of them, under the command of Haldene, their chieftain, marched into Northumberland, where they fixed their quarters; part of them took quarters at Cambridge; whence they dislodged, in the ensuing summer, and seized Wereham, in the county of Dorset, the very centre of Alfred's dominions. That prince so straitened them in these quarters, that they were content to come to a treaty with him, and stipulated to depart his country. Alfred, well acquainted with their usual perfidy, obliged them to swear, upon the holy reliques, to the observance of the treaty; not that he expected they would pay any veneration to the reliques; but he hoped, if they now violated this oath, their impiety would draw down upon them the vengeance of heaven. But the Danes. little apprehensive of the danger, suddenly, without seeking any pretence, fell upon Alfred's army; and having put it to rout, marched westward, and took possession of Exeter.

The king collected new forces; and exerted such vigour, that he fought, in one year, eight battles with the enemy, and reduced them to the utmost extremity. He hearkened, however, to new proposals of peace, and was satisfied to stipulate with them, that they would settle somewhere in England, and would not permit more ravagers into the kingdom. But while he was expecting the execution of this treaty, which it seemed the interest of the Danes themselves to fulfil, he heard that another body had landed; and, having collected all the scattered troops of their countrymen, had surprized Chippenham, then a considerable town, and were exercising their usual ravages all around them.

This

This last incident quite broke through the spirit of the Saxons, and reduced them to despair. Finding that, after all the miserable havoc which they had undergone in their persons and in their property; after all the vigorous actions which they had exerted in their own defence; a new band, equally greedy of spoil and slaughter, had disembarked among them; they believed themselves abandoned by heaven to destruction, and delivered over to those swarms of robbers, which the fertile north thus incessantly poured forth against them. Some left their country, and retired into Wales, or fled beyond sea; others submitted to the conquerors, in hopes of appeasing their fury by a servile obedience: And every man's attention being now engrossed in concern for his own preservation, no one would hearken to the exhortation of the king, who summoned them to make under his conduct one effort more in defence of their prince, their country, and their liberties. Alfred himself was obliged to relinquish the ensigns of his dignity, to dismiss his servants, and seek shelter in the meanest disguises, from the pursuit and fury of his enemies.

He concealed himself under a peasant's habit, and lived in the house of a neat-herd who had been entrusted with the care of some of his cows. There passed here an incident, which has been recorded by all the historians, and was long preserved by popular tradition, though it contains nothing memorable in itself, except so far as every circumstance is interesting which attends so much virtue and dignity reduced to such distress. The wife of the neat-herd was ignorant of the rank of her royal guest; and observing him one day busy by the fire side, trimming his bow and arrows, she desired him to take care of some cakes which were toasting, while she was employed elsewhere in other domestic affairs. But Alfred, whose thoughts were otherwise engaged, neglected this injunction; and the good woman, on her return, finding her cakes all burnt, rated the king very severely,

and

and upbraided him, that he always seemed well pleased to eat her warm cakes, though he was so negligent in toasting them.

By degrees, Alfred, as he found the search of the enemy become more remiss, collected some of his retainers, and retired into the centre of a bog, formed by the stagnating waters of the Thone and Parret, in Somersetshire. He here found two acres of firm ground, and building a habitation on them, rendered himself secure by its fortifications; and still more, by the unknown and inaccessible roads which led to it, and by the forests and morasses with which it was every way environed. This place he called Æthelingay, or the Isle of Nobles, and it now bears the name of Athelney. He thence made frequent and unexpected sallies upon the Danes, who often felt the vigour of his arm, but knew not from what quarter the blow came. He subsisted himself and his followers, by the plunder which he acquired; and, from small successes, he opened their minds to hope, that notwithstanding his present low condition, more important victories might, at length, attend his valour.

Alfred lay here concealed, but not inactive, during a twelve month; when the news of a prosperous event reached his ears, and called him to the field. Ubba, the Dane, having spread devastation, fire and slaughter, over Wales, had landed in Devonshire, from twenty-three vessels; and laid siege to the castle of Kinwith, a place situated near the mouth of the small river Tan. Oddune, earl of Devonshire, with his followers, had taken shelter there; and being ill supplied with provisions, and even with water, he determined, by some vigorous blow, to prevent the necessity of submitting to the barbarous enemy.

He made a sudden sally on the Danes; and, taking them unprepared, he put them to the rout, pursued them with
great

great slaughter, killed Ubba himself, and got possession of the famous Reafen, or enchanted standard, in which the Danes put great confidence. It contained the figure of a raven, which had been woven by three sisters of Hingnar and Ubba, with many magical incantations; and which, by its different movements, prognosticated, as the Danes believed, the good or bad success of any enterprize.

When Alfred observed this symptom of successful resistance in his subjects, he left his retreat; but before he would assemble them in arms, or urge them to any attempt, which, if unfortunate, might, in their present despondency, prove fatal; he resolved to inspect himself, the situation of the enemy, and to judge of the probability of success. For this purpose he entered their camp, under the disguise of a harper, and passed unsuspected through every quarter. He so entertained them with his music and facetious humours, that he met with a welcome reception; and was even introduced to the tent of Guthrum, their prince, where he remained some days.

He remarked the supine security of the Danes, their contempt of the English, their negligence in foraging and plundering, and their dissolute wasting of what they gained by rapine and violence. Encouraged by these favourable appearances, he secretly sent emissaries to the most considerable of his subjects, and summoned them to a rendezvous, attended by their warlike followers, at Brixton, on the borders of Selwood Forest. The English, who had hoped to put an end to their calamities, by servile submission, now found the insolence and rapine of the conqueror more intolerable than all past fatigues and dangers; and at the appointed day they joyfully resorted to their prince. On his appearance, they received him with shouts of applause, and could not satiate their eyes with the sight of this beloved monarch, whom they had long regarded as dead, and who

G

now,

now, with voice and look, expreſſing his confidence of ſucceſs, called them to liberty, and to vengeance. He inſtantly conducted them to Eddington, where the Danes were encamped; and taking advantage of his previous knowledge of the place, he directed his attack againſt the moſt unguarded quarter of the enemy.

THE Danes, ſurprized to ſee an army of Engliſh, whom they conſidered as totally ſubdued, and ſtill more aſtoniſhed to hear that Alfred was at their head, made but a faint reſiſtance, notwithſtanding their ſuperior number; and were ſoon put to flight, with great ſlaughter. The remainder of the routed army, with their prince, was beſieged by Alfred, in a fortified camp, to which they fled; but being reduced to extremity, by want and hunger, they had recourſe to the clemency of the victor, and offered to ſubmit on any conditions. The king, no leſs generous than brave, gave them their lives; and even formed a ſcheme for converting them from mortal enemies, into faithful ſubjects and confederates. He knew that the kingdoms of Eaſt Anglia and Northumberland were totally deſolated, by the frequent inroads of the Danes; and he now propoſed to repeople them, by ſettling there, Guthrum and his followers.

IN this interval of tranquility, the king inſtituted civil and military inſtitutions. He ordained, that all his people ſhould be armed and regiſtered; he aſſigned them a regular rotation of duty; he diſtributed part into the caſtles and fortreſſes which he built at proper places; he required another part to take the field on any alarm, and to aſſemble at ſtated places of rendezvous; and, he left a ſufficient number at home, who were employed in the cultivation of the land, and who afterwards took their turn in military ſervice. The whole kingdom was like one great garriſon; and the Danes ould no ſooner appear in one place, than a ſufficient number

was

was affembled to oppofe them, without leaving the other defencelefs or difarmed.

But Alfred, fenfible that the proper method of oppofing an enemy, who made incurfions by fea, was to meet them on their own element, took care to provide himfelf with a naval force, which, though the moft natural defence of an ifland, had hitherto been totally neglected by the Englifh. He increafed the fhipping of his kingdom, both in number and ftrength, and trained his fubjects in the practice, as well of failing as of naval action. He diftributed his armed veffels in proper ftations, around the ifland, and was fure to meet the Danifh fhips, either before or after they had landed their troops, and to purfue them in all their incurfions. Though the Danes might fuddenly difembark on the coaft, which was generally become defolate, by their frequent ravages, they were encountered by the Englifh fleet in their retreat, and efcaped not as formerly, by abandoning their booty; but paid, by their total deftruction, the penalty of the diforders which they had committed.

In this manner, Alfred repelled feveral inroads of thefe piratical Danes, and maintained his kingdom during fome years, in fafety and tranquility. A fleet of 120 fhips of war was ftationed upon the coaft; and being provided with warlike engines, as well as with expert feamen, both Frifians and Englifh, for Alfred fupplied the defects of his own fubjects by engaging able foreigners in his fervice, maintained fuperiority over thofe fmaller bands, with which England had fo often been infefted. But at laft, Haftings, the famous Danifh chief, having ravaged all the provinces of France, both along the fea coaft, and the Loire and Seine, and being obliged to quit that country, more by the defolation which he himfelf had occafioned, than by the refiftance of the inhabitants, appeared off Kent, with a fleet of 330 fail. The greater part of the enemy difembarked in the

Rother, and seized the fort of Apuldore. Hastings himself, commanding a fleet of eighty sail, entered the Thames, and fortifying Milton, in Kent, began to spread his forces over the country, and to commit the most destructive ravages.

But Alfred, on the first alarm of this descent, flew to the defence of his people, at the head of a select band of soldiers, whom he always kept about his person; and gathering to him the armed militia from all quarters, appeared in the field with a force superior to the enemy. All straggling parties, whom necessity, or love of plunder, had drawn to a distance from their chief encampment, were cut off by the English; and these pirates, instead of increasing their spoil, found themselves cooped up in their fortifications, and obliged to live on the plunder they had brought from France. Tired of this situation, which must in the end prove ruinous to them, the Danes, at Apuldore, rose suddenly from their encampment, with an intention of marching towards the Thames, and passing over into Essex; but they escaped not the vigilance of Alfred, who encountered them at Farnham, and put them to rout; seized all their horses and baggage, and chaced the runaways on board their ships, which carried them up the Colne to Mersey, in Essex, where they entrenched themselves. Hastings, at the same time, and probably by concert, made a like movement; and, deserting Milton, took possession of Bamflete, near the isle of Canvey, in the same county, where he hastily threw up fortifications for his defence, against the power of Alfred.

Unfortunately for the English, Guthrum, prince of the East Anglian Danes, was dead; as was also Guthred, whom the king had appointed governor of the Northumbrians; and those restless tribes, being no longer restrained by the authority of their princes, and being encouraged by the appearance of a considerable body of their countrymen, broke into rebellion, shook off the authority

of

of Alfred, and yielding to their inveterate habits of war and depredation, embarked on board 240 veffels, and appeared before Exeter. Alfred loft not a moment in oppofing this new enemy. Having left fome forces at London, to make head againft Haftings and the other Danes, he marched fuddenly to the weft; and, falling on the rebels before they were aware, purfued them to their ships with great flaughter. Thefe ravagers, failing next to Suffex, began to plunder the country near Chichefter; but the order which Alfred had every where eftablifhed, fufficed here without his prefence, for the defence of the place; and, the rebels meeting with a new repulfe, in which many of them were killed, and fome of their fhips taken, were obliged to put again to fea, and were difcouraged from attempting any other enterprize.

MEANWHILE, the Danifh invaders in Effex, having united their force, under the command of Haftings, advanced into their inland country, and made fpoil of all around them; but foon had reafon to repent their temerity. The Englifh army left in London, affifted by a body of citizens, attacked the enemy's entrenchments at Banflete, overpowered the garrifon, and having done great execution upon them, carried off the wife and two fons of Haftings. Alfred generoufly fpared thefe captives, and even reftored them to Haftings, on condition that he fhould depart the kingdom.

BUT though the king had thus honourably rid himfelf of this dangerous enemy, he had not entirely fubdued or expelled the invaders. The piratical Danes, willingly followed in an excurfion any profperous leader who gave them hopes of booty; but were not fo eafily induced to relinquifh their enterprize, or fubmit to return, baffled and without plunder, into their native country. Great numbers

of

of them, after the departure of Hastings, seized and fortified Shobury, at the mouth of the Thames; and having left a garrison there, they marched along the river till they came to Bodinton, in the county of Glocester; where, being reinforced by some Welsh, they threw up entrenchments, and prepared for their defence. The king here surrounded them with the whole force of his dominions; and, as he had now a certain prospect of victory, he resolved to trust nothing to chance, but rather to master his enemies by famine than assault.

They were so reduced that having eaten their horses, and having many of them perished with hunger, they made a desperate sally upon the English; and, though the greater number fell in the action, a considerable number escaped. These roved about in England, for some time, still pursued by the vigilance of Alfred; they attacked Leicester with success, defended themselves in Hartford, and then fled to Quatford, where they were finally broken and subdued.

The small remains of these Danes, either dispersed themselves among their countrymen, in Northumberland and East Anglia, or had recourse again to the sea, where they exercised piracy, under the command of Sigefort, a Northumbrian. This freebooter, well acquainted with Alfred's naval preparations, had framed vessels on a new construction; being higher and longer, as well as swifter, than those of the English; but the king soon discovered his superior skill, by building vessels still higher, longer, and swifter, than those of the Northumbrians; and falling upon them while they were exercising their ravages in the west, he took twenty of their ships; and having tried all the prisoners at Winchester, he hanged them as pirates, the common enemies of mankind.

The

The well-timed severity of this execution, together with the excellent posture of defence, established every where, restored full tranquility in England; and provided, for the future, security of the government. The East Anglian and Northumbrian Danes, on the first appearance of Alfred upon their frontiers, made anew the most humble submissions to him; and he thought it prudent to take them under his immediate government, without establishing over them a viceroy of their own nation.

Previous to the time of Alfred, and during that admirable reign, we have dwelt rather minutely on the Danish Invasions; but as, at his death, the Danes inhabited nearly the one half of England, their future skirmishes and battles may be rather said to be incursions in a country which they partly possessed, than invasions on a strange territory; therefore it would not be consistent with our plan, that only professes to give a History of Invasions, to enlarge it by a history of every battle, when not preceded by invasion.

The Danes continued to plunder and harrass the country, with their usual barbarity, from the death of Alfred, till the end of the reign of Ethelred II. a period of 113 years; at this time, they had conquered the greatest part of England; and Ethelred flying to Normandy with his family, Sweyn, king of Denmark, was proclaimed king of England.

Ethelred was conquered by the Danes, chiefly through the *treachery* of one of his subjects, Edric, Duke of Mercia. This arch traitor, held a *secret correspondence* with the enemy,

enemy, while he *pretended* THE PUREST PATRIOTISM. Although his treasons were several times pardoned by Ethelred, and his son and successor, Edmund Ironside, he was still detected in fresh conspiracies against his native country, and its princes. But at length, he was justly put to death, by Canute the Great, who even detested the parricide that had enabled him and his father, Sweyn, to mount the throne of England, by betraying the interests of that country.

ETHELRED, before his departure for Normandy, addressed some of his nobility in a very pathetic manner. He alluded thus, to the *treasons* of Edric and *others*:

" WE are not overcome by the swords, or courage of
" the enemy, *but by the* TREASON *and* PERFIDY *of our*
" FRIENDS. *Our navy is betrayed into the hands of the*
" *Danes; our armies are betrayed by the revolt of most of our*
" *officers;* our DESIGNS *betrayed to the enemy, by our coun-*
" *sellors, who, instead of extricating us from our troubles,*
" *are continually persuading us to* INFAMOUS TREATIES!
" *and your valour and loyalty is rendered ineffectual, by the*
" *treachery of your leaders.*"

ON the death of Sweyn, who did not survive a twelve-month after he mounted the throne of England, two powerful factions divided the nation: the one consisted of Danes, and those English, who were well affected to them. The other was formed of the English nobles and commons, who were disaffected to the Danish government, and wished to throw off so disagreeable a yoke. The former immediately proclaimed Canute, the son of Sweyn, king of England. The latter recalled Ethelred.

As Canute fled to Denmark, Ethelred remounted the throne. But the Dane returning the following year with a

powerful

powerful armament, he invaded the southern coast, and in little more than a year, by the deaths of Ethelred and his son, Edmund, and Canute's own bravery, he was acknowledged king of all England.

Two more Danish princes, besides Canute, swayed the English Sceptre, till the restoration of the Saxon line; when all distinctions, between the two nations, gradually disappeared. The Danes were interspersed with the English, in most of the provinces; they spoke nearly the same language; they differed little in their manners and laws; while domestic dissentions, in Denmark, prevented any more powerful invasions from thence, which might awaken past animosity; and as the Norman conquest which ensued soon after reduced both nations to equal subjection, there is no farther mention in history of any difference between them.

CHAP. IV.

NORWEGIAN AND NORMAN INVASIONS.

ON the death of Edward the Confessor, Harold, the second son of Earl Godwin, without the least hereditary pretensions, ascended the throne of England. His family, indeed, in point of great authority, vast possessions, and powerful alliances, was the first in the kingdom; and Harold had the policy, in the life-time of Edward, to render himself so popular, that he set aside Elgar Atheling, the lineal heir, in favour of himself, without any disturbance or murmurs.

The Duke of Normandy, nearly related to the Confessor's mother, and who is reported to have been left his successor, by the will of Edward, when he heard of Harold's intrigues, and accession, was moved to the highest pitch of indignation. He summoned him immediately to resign the crown, which Harold refusing, it fixed William in the resolution of invading England.

It is a mistake, that the Norman language and manners were introduced into England by William. They were brought in by Edward the Confessor, who was educated in Normandy, and had contracted such an intimacy with the natives, and an affection for their manners, as soon rendered their language, customs, and laws, fashionable throughout the kingdom. The study of the French tongue
became

became general among the people; and the courtiers affected to imitate the Normans in their dress, equipage, and entertainments. Even the lawyers employed that language in their deeds and papers, and the greatest church dignities were bestowed on the Norman clergy. This previous fashionable partiality for the laws, manners, and language of Normandy, must have induced the Britons to submit to William, after the death of Harold, with the greater facility, which was chiefly owing to the clergy; some of them, perhaps, being either Normans themselves, or had been educated or patronized by those of that nation, who came over with Edward the Confessor.

William assembled a fleet of 3000 sail. The ships were made with flat bottoms, to draw but little water, and suitable to the purposes of carrying both men and horses. He had selected an army of 60,000 men. The camp bore a splendid, yet a martial appearance, from the discipline of the men, the beauty and vigour of the horses, the lustre of the arms, and the accoutrements of both; but, above all, from the high names of nobility who engaged under the banners of the Duke of Normandy. To these bold chieftains, the issue of which now compose our greatest families, William held up the spoils of England, as the prize of their valour; and, pointing to the opposite shore, called to them, prophetically, that there was the field on which they must erect trophies to their name, and fix their establishments.

While he was making these mighty preparations, that he might increase the number of Harold's enemies, he excited the inveterate rancour of Tosti, brother of Harold, and encouraged him, with the King of Norway, to infest the coasts of England. His design was, to make a diversion in the east, while he effected a landing in the south.

NORWEGIAN INVASION.

The King of Norway appeared at the mouth of the Humber, with a fleet of 300 sail. William had before this, entrusted Tosti with sixty ships and a body of troops, preparatory to the grand blow, in order to harrass the English coast, and sound the affections of the people. He ravaged the Isle of Wight, and scoured the coast, but was at last driven back to his ships with great slaughter, several of which were burnt. After sailing to Scotland, to solicit the aid of Malcolm, the successor of Macbeth, he joined the Norwegian monarch, off the Humber. The two fleets sailed up the river, where they landed their forces, and immediately marched forwards to lay siege to the city of York.

This invasion was so sudden and unexpected, that the Earls Edwin and Morcar, who were the governors of that country, had not time to levy a sufficient force to dispute their landing; however, knowing that something must be done in this critical situation, in order to check the enemy in their progress, till a stronger reinforcement could be sent from the southern parts of the kingdom, they got together a few troops from the adjacent countries, and advanced to oppose the invaders; but these troops, consisting of raw undisciplined men, were quickly beaten; and the enemy proceeding onwards, sat down before the city of York, which soon fell a prey to them, where they put the greatest part of the inhabitants to the sword.

On the first news of the King of Norway's descent, Harold marched with a chosen body of veteran troops to oppose him, but could not come up time enough to prevent the

the fate of York. At length, however, the two armies met near Standford Brigg, since called Battle Bridge, which bridge was guarded by a party of Norwegians, who defended it for some time with great intrepidity; and being driven from it, the action became general, and was obstinately maintained by both parties, till victory at length declared in favour of the English. The loss of the invaders was almost incredible; amongst others, their leaders Harfagar and Tosti, were left dead on the field of battle, and a very considerable booty fell into the hands of the conquerors.

HAROLD, wisely pursuing this advantage, made himself master of many of the Norwegian ships; but at length coming to an agreement with Paul, count of the Orkneys, and Olans, the son of the Norway King, he suffered them to carry off their wounded, in twenty one ships, on their swearing never more to invade the dominion of England.

THE Defeat of the Norwegians, and death of Tosti, greatly disconcerted the Duke of Normandy; but his resolution, which never forsook him, determined him to pursue his preparations with redoubled vigour, and to obtain the crown of England, or perish in the attempt.

THE emperor, Henry IV. by the advice of the imperial council, issued a proclamation, permitting any of the vassals and dependents of the empire to enter into the service of William. The court of France, however, gave him no manner of encouragement to prosecute his enterprize; but advised, or rather commanded him, as a vassal, not to enter into it.

BUT this discountenance of the Gallic court, was overbalanced by the favour and protection of Pope Alexander the II. who, upon William's promising to hold England as a fief of the Apostolic See, immediately excommunicated

Harold,

Harold, pronounced him a perjured traitor, and an ufurper and fent to the Duke of Normandy a ring, with one of St. Peter's hairs in it, and a confecrated banner.

He likewife publifhed bulls, to fanctify William's caufe, and invited all Chriftians to affift in placing him on the throne of England. Thefe concurrent circumftances not only roufed many foreigners to join the Norman ftandard, but numbers of the Englifh themfelves, looking upon Harold as an excommunicated perfon, deferted him, and joined the enemy of their country.

NORMAN INVASION.

At length the Duke of Normandy fet fail from St. Valery, in the year 1066, on the eve of the feaft of St. Michael, the tutelary faint of the Normans; and landed, without oppofition, the next day, at Pevenfy, in Suffex, having loft in his paffage only two fmall veffels, that were overladen.

The duke is faid to have been himfelf the firft who jumped afhore, and the writers of his life have, upon this occafion, adapted to him an incident we meet with in the life of Julius Cæfar; for they tell us, that his foot flipping he fell down, when a foldier ftanding by, immediately turned it into a good omen; faying, "Sir, you have thus "taken feizen of that land of which you will fhortly be "king."

After William had thus effected a landing, he acted with the moft refined policy, by returning, or as others

fay,

say, with greater probability, by sending his fleet back to Normandy, that his men might be deprived of any hopes of personal safety, but by victory; then marching to Hastings, in Sussex, he erected a fortification, and publishing a manifesto, containing his reasons for undertaking this enterprize; and setting forth, that he came to revenge the death of Prince Alfred, restore Robert, archbishop of Canterbury, and assist the English in punishing Harold; who had seized the crown to which he had no right, in direct violation of the oath he had sworn at the Norman court. But these reasons were treated as frivolous, by every Englishman of good sense; for, in the first place, Alfred had fallen by Godwin, who had been tried and fined for the same; but although that punishment fell far short of the crime, yet Harold could not be involved in the guilt, as it did not appear that he had any hand in the murder.

The second reason was no better than the first, though probably inserted in the manifesto, on the Pope's account, to serve as a cover for his partiality to the duke; for it was well known that prelate had been banished, by the general assembly of the kingdom, in Edward's reign, and consequently the present king could not be blamed for it; moreover, it was in itself a wise and justifiable measure, and such as was universally approved of by the English themselves. Thirdly, as to his offering the English his assistance, to bring Harold to condign punishment, for having seized the crown without right, and in direct contravention to his oath; Harold had fully answered every thing that William could alledge on that subject.

What most surprized all thinking people was, that William, in his manifesto, never mentioned, or even hinted, at any will made by the deceased King Edward;

we

we may therefore venture to suppose, that neither will or verbal promise had been made; and that the Duke of Normandy, in reality, had smaller pretensions to the crown of England than even Harold.

It is to be observed, that a political step of William's was of infinite service to his cause; for when his provisions were consumed, he gave strict orders that his people should not plunder the inhabitants, in order to procure any more.

By this prudent step, he in all probability, saved his army from destruction; for the inhabitants of the adjacent country, finding themselves treated thus mildly, endeavoured to secure the favour and protection of their new master, by supplying him with all those necessaries which he wanted, instead of retiring with their effects, cattle, &c. up the country; which a contrary conduct would certainly have occasioned.

About this time, a Norman baron, named Robert, who had been for some time settled in the northern parts of England, sent William an account of Harold's victory over the King of Norway, and his return from the north to London; advising him, at the same time, not to venture a battle with such a numerous army of brave men as the usurper had to bring against him; but rather to entrench himself as strong as possible in his camp, at Hastings.

William, however, either too judicious, or too intrepid, to follow such timorous advice, returned for answer, " That he was come into England to seek his enemy; that " he put confidence in the valour of his troops, and did not " doubt of success; and that he held it beneath the honour " of a general, who had the swords of 60,000 brave men " unsheathed in his cause, to waste time in parlying."

Harold

HAROLD, in this exigency, made a general muster of his forces; and found, too late, the bad effects of his ill-timed parsimony; the consequences of which he strove to repair, by the kindest behaviour to those who remained firm to him; and by soliciting the assistance of the nobles of the kingdom, to whom he represented the danger to which they, their country, and himself were exposed. Many of the nobility accordingly joined him, or sent him succours; and in the interim, William sent ambassadors to demand the crown, which he accused him of having perfidiously and perjuriously usurped.

HAROLD, enraged at such an haughty and insolent message, returned an answer, teeming with equal asperity of language; and strained every nerve to oppose the Normans with vigour. Some of the English nobles, however, strove to mitigate that martial fire, with which Harold seemed to be animated, and persuaded him to make this proposition to William: That if he would depart the kingdom quietly, the expences of his expedition should be defrayed. The Norman received this overture with the contempt it merited, and returned this answer:

" THAT he was not come over for the sake of plunder or
" paltry coin, but to seize that kingdom which was his
" due; and which Harold, in violation of the most sacred
" oaths, had usurped; and that nothing else would satisfy
" him." Upon the receipt of this answer, Harold, who it seems thought too lightly of his enemy, with respect to number, skill, and courage, marched towards the Normans, and encamped within seven miles of Hastings. While the two armies were thus situated, Gyrth, one of Harold's brothers, who was equally remarkable for his courage and prudence, represented to the king, that the wisest step he could take, would be to temporize and procrastinate coming to an engagement; remonstrating,

" THAT

" THAT all his supplies were not yet come up; that the
" enemy was therefore much superior in number; that his
" army was fatigued with its march; and that it would be
" better to content himself with wasting the country, and
" carrying off all the provisions it afforded, till the expected
" succours should join him from the north; that such a con-
" duct would greatly distress the enemy, who, when they
" found that they could neither subsist in the country, nor
" force the issue of a battle, would be glad to come into
" any terms, to secure a safe retreat, and leave the land with
" more precipitation than they ever entered it." At the
same time he besought his brother to let him take the command of the army on himself.

" RESERVE yourself, (said this able counsellor,) to other
" times; while you are safe, the enemy can never be said to
" conquer; but on your person, the fate of your kingdom
" depends. Leave me to fight the Normans, if by chance
" a favourable occasion shall offer, while you keep yourself
" ready to reap the glory of my success, or repair the mis-
" fortune of my defeat."

BUT Harold was unfortunately deaf to this salutary advice; till the next day, when, in company with Gyrth,
he reconnoitered the enemy's camp, and found them far
from being so contemptible as his sanguine imagination
had represented them. Perceiving that he had been greatly
imposed upon, both with respect to their numbers and
discipline, he now proposed to retreat to London, till he
could increase his forces, and take the field against so
powerful a foe, with greater advantages to himself. But
here Gyrth again opposed his intentions; and, with a
generous warmth, told him,

" THAT he ought to have gone and abided in that city,
" agreeable to the advice of himself and others, his faith-
" ful

"ful counsellors, till the arrival of his troops; but, since
"it was now too late to repent, so it would be ignomini-
"ous to recede; that his honour was now engaged, and
"he must stand the test, prepared either to conquer, or
"lose all; that the least step towards a retreat, would be
"construed into a flight, and lose him in the opinions of
"his soldiers and all the world; animate the Normans,
"and so discourage his own men, that they would cer-
"tainly desert him, and he would never again be able
"to reassemble them."

HAROLD was convinced of the propriety of this advice; and now the impending struggle, for dominion and power, entirely engrossed his thoughts, when a Monk, named Hugh Margot, came to the English camp, on a message from William, with the four following propositions, viz. The first was, that Harold should relinquish the kingdom, upon certain conditions; the second, that he should hold it under homage to the duke; the third, that they should refer the decision of their difference to the Pope; and the fourth, to determine their quarrel by single combat, and the kingdom to be the prize of the conqueror.

To those propositions Harold replied, "That he was
"not so simple as to submit to the arbitration of the Pope,
"who had already declared himself a party; that he
"scorned to hold the crown of England, dependent on
"any prince whatever; nor would he put his kingdom on
"the issue of a single combat, in which, though he should
"obtain the victory, he could reap no solid advantage;
"and that therefore he would leave the decision of his
"cause to God alone."

THE Norman barons and officers now grew pressing to be led to engage, before Harold could receive any farther reinforcements. William was pleased with their willingness; but, at the same time, to prevent, if possible, the effusion of human blood; and to conceal his ambition, beneath the shew of reluctance, he determined to try the result of a personal conference, in which he intended to offer all the provinces of England, north of the Humber, to Harold; and to secure the Godwin patrimonial estate to Gyrth, provided all the rest of England was ceded to himself. And, in case of a refusal to these proposals, to pronounce Harold a perjured traitor; to challenge him to a general engagement; and to declare all such as should adhere to him, excommunicated by the Pope.

With this view, William advanced at the head of a select party of twenty persons only; but Harold, not chusing to enter into a personal conference with William, sent his brother Gyrth, to hear what the Duke of Normandy had to say. After the interview, Gyrth made his report to the council, of the duke's offers and threats; the latter of which, we are told, made a considerable impression upon many of the members. Perjury, and breach of promise, sounded strange and ominous to English ears; and the menace of excommunication, carried with it a force only to be conceived by those who live under the terror of ecclesiastical rule, or are the dupes of bigotry and religious superstition.

The assembly, therefore, unanimously advised Harold to come to an accommodation; but Gyrth, alarmed at, though unaffected with the panic, which had now diffused itself like a contagion, from the council to the army, resolved to exert his utmost efforts to stop the spreading poison to their hopes; and, with irresistable eloquence, displayed to them the certain loss of honour, power, possessions, liberty; in a word, of every thing dear to a freeborn Englishman, that would await so pusillanimous a resolution; expatiating on the miseries they had to expect,

under

under the rule of a conqueror, who had already devoted their persons and effects, as a prey to those who assisted him in the conquest.

This harangue had the intended effect, and inspired the hearers with an enthusiastic desire to appeal to the decision of the sword. Harold, to take the advantage of this propensity, appointed the ensuing day, October 14th, 1066, which happened to be his birth-day, for a general engagement.

William, finding that Harold designed to give him battle, posted himself advantageously on an open plain, and obliged his troops to pass the preceding night in sobriety, silence, and acts of devotion. While, on the contrary, riot and confusion reigned in the English camp. Harold, flushed with his late success against the Norwegians, and pleased with the apparent order of his troops, appeared rather too confident of victory; and seemed to be previously secure of what, upon all such sanguine occasions, is in the power of Providence alone to bestow. Such were the hopes and the behaviour of the adverse parties, previous to the engagement; but, of the battle itself, the subsequent is the most ample, and the best account extant.

Harold, far inferior in the number of his forces, resolved not to lose any advantage in the ground; and therefore drew up his men on the brow of a hill, with a ditch and a line of hurdles before them. The Kentish men, armed with halberts, pikes, and targets, formed the van, a post of honour, which they claimed as their right, by antient usage, ever since the time of the Saxon Heptarchy. The care of defending the king's person, and the royal standard, was, by like prescription, consigned to the

Londoners,

Londoners, whom Harold particularly cautioned to keep close together; telling them, that breaking their ranks would be attended with inevitable difcomfiture. Thefe latter formed the main body, and the remaining ranks were indifcriminately filled up with the other Englifh.

Harold, and his brother Gyrth, and Leafwine, placed themfelves in the centre, that their men might be witneffes of their valour; and, difdaining an indulgence that was not fhared by the meaneft foldier, they fought on foot. The whole together formed a well-compacted phalanx, whofe clofe cemented ranks feemed indiffoluble, by any force that could affail them.

William, mounting on horfeback, encouraged his men with a voice that feemed to breathe victory; he appealed to heaven for the juftnefs of his caufe; he then hung round his neck, as witneffes of his rivals perjury, the relics on which Harold had fworn; and ordered the confecrated banner, fent him by the Pope, to be unfurled in the front of his army. Thefe things, which would be laughed to fcorn in the prefent enlightened times, had a wonderful effect in thofe days of dark ignorance and blind fuperftition.

The Normans thought they marched under the protection of heaven. They advanced in three bodies; the firft compofed of the troops of Bretagne, Anjou, Le Maine, and Perche, led by Fitz-Ofbern, and Roger de Montgomery; the fecond, of Poictevins and Germans, under the command of Charles Martel, and a German general; the duke himfelf led up the laft divifion, confifting of his own Normans, and the flower of his nobility; and among all the three divifions, were interfperfed flying bodies of archers, to ferve as opportunity fhould offer.

The

The Normans, marching with the Pope's banner at their head, to begin the attack on three sides at once, Taillefer, a gallant old soldier, advanced before the rest, and sung, according to custom, the famous song of Roland, and the heroes who fell at Ronceval, to rouze the valour of his countrymen. To animate them still more, by his example, he obtained the duke's permission to strike the first blow in the battle; upon which he rushed on to begin the charge, running a standard-bearer through with his lance, and killing another with his sword; but before he could dispatch a third, he himself was slain.

The air was now darkened by a cloud of arrows, discharged from the bows of the Norman archers, which greatly disordered the English; who, seeing their men fall on all sides, thought the centre of their army had been broken through; which, for a while, occasioned such a confusion and dismay, as was easily perceived by the Normans; who, resolving to follow their advantage, charged with redoubled impetuosity; but the English, having recovered from their first astonishment, and forming a penthouse with their targets over their heads, closed their ranks, and presented such an impenetrable body to their enemy, as obliged them to retire; and thus reunited, did amazing execution with their javelins; insomuch, that the troops in the left wing, giving way, were pushed into some covered ditches, which they had not observed, as they marched up to the attack. The other corps being struck with a panic, on a false report that the duke was slain, were preparing for flight; when he, coming up in lucky time, shewed them their mistake, rallied them, and led them again to the fight.

The English, vain of this trifling advantage, had, contrary to Harold's express command, quitted their post on the hill, to pursue the broken columns into the plain; which,

which, as soon as William perceived, he, with a happy readiness, brought up a body of Norman cavalry from his right wing, and cut off the retreat of 3000 of the most advanced of the pursuers; consisting of the Kentish and Essex men, all of whom he put to the sword.

He then renewed the general attack against the main body of the English, by whom he was received with the same firmness and intrepidity as before. He was repulsed on all sides; and, wherever he strove to make an impression, the loss reverted upon himself. Thus circumstanced, he despaired of prevailing by open force. Thrice had he led up the charge, and each time the horse, on which he rode, was killed. He flew from rank to rank, from squadron to squadron; animating, by his words, and encouraging, by his example, both the brave and irresolute; sometimes rushing on with a torrent of death in his rear, sometimes opposing his single authority to a crowd of runaways.

Harold, with equal spirit, with equal valour, but with superior success, opposed him. The eyes of his faithful English were fixed upon him. By his uplifted sword, he dealt the blow, and mowed down the remaining ranks which his javelin had thinned; no man felt fatigue, no man thought of recess, while their king seemed lost to every sense, but that of a thirst for glory; and to have nothing in pursuit, but conquest or death.

And now victory appeared on the point of passing over to the side of the English; the drooping Normans staggered under the resistless shock, when William's genius found means to fix the wavering fortune of the day, by one of those stratagems in war, which, from their frequency, are the less suspected or guarded against. He sounded a retreat. It proved the knell of English liberty!

Harold's

Harold's brave troops, thinking that nothing now remained but to glean the deathful harvest for which they had so painfully laboured, were ruined by a rash security. Deaf to all order, impetuous, and ungovernable, they pursued the wily fugitives into the plain, with as little caution as before; and they who, when united, were invincible, when thus dispersed, became an easy prey to those whom they were too confident of having vanquished. For the Normans, rallying upon a signal given, closed their ranks, faced about, and surrounding their pursuers with their cavalry, cut numbers of them in pieces; and the rest, with great difficulty regained the hill, where they still maintained their ground, in spite of the utmost efforts of the enemy to dislodge them or break their ranks.

The Normans, finding all their attacks fruitless, had recourse to their former stratagem; and, amazing to be told! it met with the same success. The English, never to be taught by experience, when their fighting humour is indulged, forgot the check they had so lately met with; and followed the enemy, a third time, into the plain, where they were again trodden down by the Norman horses, and the field strewed with their dead bodies.

Weakened, as they were, with these repeated losses, they still kept their ground upon the hill, unshaken, for some time; and, in all probability, might have recovered their strength and spirits; and have finally repulsed their fierce assailants; had not an arrow, shot from the bow of the evil genius of England, laid their monarch breathless on the ground, whose dying groan was the departing sigh of English liberty. William and slavery triumphed.

Gyrth and Leofwine, the gallant brothers of Harold, still survived, and still animated their countrymen to stand

their

their ground. The amazed English thronged, instinctively, round the standard of their deceased prince; but the Normans, pouring upon them in redoubled numbers, carried their point; Gyrth and Leofwine fell in each others arms; Harold's standard was pulled down, and the duke's erected in its stead; upon which the English retired from all parts of the hill, and were hotly pursued by the enemy, even after the close of the day.

The darkness, however, which favoured their retreat, had well nigh proved fatal to the Normans, by wresting the victory out of their hands. For, in the eagerness of their pursuit, and not being so well acquainted with the country as the English, they fell into morasses and deep ditches, and lost a great number, both of horse and foot. The fugitives, reanimated by this accident that had befallen the foe, turned upon their pursuers, and made a dreadful slaughter amongst them; Egenouf, Baron de l'Aigle, falling among the rest; and, indeed, so hot was the action, that Eustace, count of Boulogne, persuaded William to sound a retreat for that night, and not to trust to the chance of darkness, a victory that would be insured to him by the returning day.

While he was whispering this counsel in William's ear, he received a blow between his shoulders, which, for a while, bereft him of speech. The duke, however, resolving not to leave his victory imperfect, still continued the fight; the battle seemed now to be renewed; the Normans, redoubling their efforts, but still the English maintained their ground. At length, William, pretending to be touched with the fate of those he now looked upon rather as his subjects than his enemies, but in reality being fearful of experiencing one of those sudden reverses of fortune which are so frequent in battle, ordered a truce to the combat, and offered liberty for that body of English

to

to retire. This was accepted; they drew off, through the marshy defiles before mentioned; and, night being now pretty far advanced, William saw himself left in full possession of the field of battle, and of the crown of England.

Thus ended this bloody engagement, which decided the fate of England. The loss of the Normans is said to have been about 15,000 men; but of the English, a much greater number were killed.

After the battle, William ordered all his troops to kneel down on the bloody field, and return thanks to God for their success. The ensuing day was spent in burying the dead; when the body of Harold, being, with some difficulty, discovered, we are told that a Norman soldier, who was present, in a fit of unmanly exultation, struck his spear into the thigh of the dead king; which action being told the duke, he instantly ordered the base wretch to receive the punishment due to so dastardly a deed, and dismissed him from his service. He afterwards sent the bodies of the king and his brothers, to their mother Gutha, who gave them as honorable a burial as circumstances would permit, in Waltham Abbey, which had been founded by Harold himself.

Thus fell the gallant Harold, after a reign of nine months, one week, and two days. He was of a comely person, and majestic presence, which awed the beholder into a kind of veneration, and inspired all who saw him with respect. He possessed great courage; and his few faults were over-balanced by many shining virtues, and great qualities.

Though the loss which the English had sustained in the fatal battle of Hastings, was great, it might have been repaired by a great nation, *where the people were generally armed*, and where there resided so many powerful noblemen in every province, who could have assembled their retainers,

retainers, and have obliged William to divide his army, and probably to waste it in a variety of actions and rencounters.

It was thus, that the kingdom had formerly resisted, for many years, its invaders; and had been gradually subdued by the continual efforts of the Romans, Saxons, and Danes; and equal difficulties might have been apprehended by the Duke of Normandy, in this bold and hazardous invasion. But there were circumstances which rendered it difficult for the English to defend their liberties, in this critical emergency.

Great dissentions were prevalent in their counsels, and factions ran high throughout the country. Many of the dignified clergy, who biassed the people, were Normans themselves, and favourable to William. As the Danes and Saxons were now intermixed, and as the Normans were originally Danes also, it is not unlikely that a great part of the nation considered the conqueror and his followers but as another colony of their own countrymen; and this consideration might tend much to facilitate his quietly mounting the throne of England. Besides, the people, by their recent and long subjection to the Danes, had lost *all national pride and spirit;* and they regarded, therefore, with the less terror, the ignominy of another foreign yoke; and basely deemed the inconvenience of submission less formidable, than those of bloodshed, war, and resistance.

CHAP. V.

OF FRENCH AND SPANISH EARLY ATTEMPTS AT INVASION.

THE English, before the reign of William, were in general, a rude, uncultivated people; ignorant of letters, unskilled in the mechanical arts, addicted to intemperance, riot, and disorder. But what is called the conquest, put them in a situation of receiving, slowly, from abroad, the rudiments of science and cultivation; and of correcting their rough and licentious manners.

WILLIAM's Invasion was the last great enterprize of the kind, which, during the course of nearly 730 years, has fully succeeded in Europe. The restless nations of the north, soon after this, seem to have learned the practice of tillage, which thenceforth kept them at home, and freed England as well as the other kingdoms of Europe, from the devastations spread over them, by those piratical invaders.

BUT though, ever since that period, invasions have not succeeded, several have been menaced, and some attempted. Indeed, since the epoch of that invasion, England, instead of being herself invaded, has carried her conquering arms into other countries. The Norman race of princes, on the throne of England, have, at different periods, not only invaded France, but subdued it.

BETWEEN

Between the time of the conqueror and the reign of Elizabeth, we read but of two great attempts, by invasion, to conquer England. They both happened in the reign of King John. As for the Invasion of Robert, in the reign of Henry I. it need scarcely be mentioned.

When the Pope pretended to dispose of the English crown, to Philip, king of France, he levied a great army; summoned all his vassals to attend him at Rouen; collected a fleet of 1700 vessels, great and small, in the sea ports of Normandy and Picardy; and actually prepared a force which seemed equal to the greatness of the enterprize.

John, on the other hand, summoned all the vassals of the crown to meet him at Dover, with their troops. He issued out orders, at the same time, that all the ships belonging to his subjects, should rendezvous at that port; and such a vast number of men and shipping were speedily assembled, that he could not maintain them all. Part of the fleet was, therefore, sent back; and after picking out 60,000 of the best disciplined and strongest of his forces, the rest were permitted to return to their homes.

The channel was covered with ships, and the opposite coasts, of both kingdoms, overspread with troops, every moment ready to enter upon action. But the English fleet, under the command of the Earl of Salisbury, the king's natural brother, received orders, though inferior in number, to attack the French in their harbours. Salisbury performed this service with so much success, that he took 300 ships, and destroyed 100 more. Philip, finding it impossible to prevent the rest from falling into the hands of the enemy, set fire to them himself, and thereby rendered it impossible for him to proceed any farther in his enterprize.

The tyranny of John, like the bigotry and arbitrary principles of the second James, forced the chiefs of the kingdom to look abroad for protection, in the person of some other branch of the royal family. In the reign of James, the nation fixed upon his nephew and son-in-law, the Prince of Orange. In the reign of John, the barons fixed upon the eldest son of Philip, of France, Prince Lewis, who only married John's niece, Blanche, of Castile. They offered to acknowledge him as their sovereign, on condition that he would rescue them from the violence of their tyrannic prince, by coming over to England, at the head of a protecting army. Philip, after obtaining hostages from the barons, for the performance of their promise, sent over a small army to their relief; and acquainted them, that his son, at the head of a more numerous body of forces, should soon follow.

John, dreading the effects of Lewis's invasion, marched down to the sea-coasts, where he took all imaginable precautions to disappoint the expectations of his enemy, by putting every place in a proper posture of defence. He even pressed all the ships in the sea-ports, opposite France, into his service; and, manning them with the greatest expedition, resolved to fight Lewis in his passage to England; but while they were waiting for the appearance of the enemy, a violent storm happened, which either sunk, or dashed to pieces, the greatest part of his fleet.

Soon after this misfortune, Lewis sailed, with a fleet of 700 ships, and landed his troops at Sandwich, without molestation. After becoming master of the southern counties, and over-running a great part of England, he was deserted by the barons; and, owing to various causes, detested by the people. One of these was, a report that Lewis meant to exterminate all the barons and their families, as traitors to their prince; and of bestowing their

estates

estates and dignities on his native subjects. This, and the cruelties committed by the French troops, who are described by the historians as an army of devils, rather than men, joined to the death of John, and Lewis's excommunication by the Pope, for setting foot in England, so much operated against him, that he was obliged, when blocked up in London, to sue for peace, and retire to France, after borrowing 5000 marks of that city, to pay his debts.

The chief cause of his retiring, however, was owing to the commanders of the fleet of the Cinque Ports, taking or sinking the greatest part of a French fleet that was sent to his relief, with a number of troops on board.

The French having eighty large ships, and the English but forty, they durst not attack them in front; but, tacking about, and getting to windward, they bore down upon them, and did vast execution with their archers. But what most contributed to their victory, was a stratagem, which actually *blinded* the enemy, and prevented them from fighting. The English commanders contrived to have a vast quantity of *quick-lime* on board, reduced to a fine powder. Being to windward of the french fleet, each ship's crew repeatedly throwing the quick-lime into the air, it was blown by the wind into the eyes of the foe, and deprived the greater part of them, of all means of perceiving their antagonists.

From this unsuccefsful invasion of Lewis, to the reign of Elizabeth, no more attempts were made on England. As for the descent of Isabella, Queen to Edward II. on the coast of Suffolk, with 3000 men from Dort; Henry of Lancaster, afterwards Henry IV. his embarkation at Nantz, with a few followers, and landing at Ravenspur, in Yorkshire; Edward

ward IV. disembarking at the same place, seventy-two years thereafter from Zealand, at the head of 2000 men; the Earl of Richmond, afterwards Henry VII. sailing from Harfleur into Normandy with a like number of men, and landing at Milford Haven; none of all these can be strictly construed into an invasion by a foreign enemy; being only successful descents on the coast, by an ambitious Queen of England, and by illustrious fugitives, or exiles.

THE SPANISH ARMADA.

The spirit of bigotry and tyranny, by which Philip II. of Spain, formerly wedded to Mary, Queen of England, was actuated; with the fraudulent maxims which governed his counsels, excited the most violent agitation among his own people; engaged him in acts of the most enormous cruelty, and threw all Europe into combustion. Slow without prudence, ambitious without enterprize, false without deceiving any body, and refined without any true judgement, he had long harboured a secret and violent desire of revenge against Elizabeth; to execute which, he formed the plan of an Invasion of England, by fitting out his invincible Armada.

He disgusted the English nation, when the husband of Mary, by his haughtiness, his reserve, and his cruelty. Although the parliament made it treason to imagine, or attempt the death of Philip, during the life of the queen, they denied their consent to his coronation, or to his being declared presumptive heir to the crown; and he could not even obtain the power of being invested with the administration of public affairs.

L

Many circumstances contributed to his hatred of Elizabeth. The rejection of his hand, on the death of her sister; and her embracing the protestant cause, which equally set at defiance his feigned love and his real chagrin: The recollection of having saved her life from the cruel bigotry of Mary, and the sanguinary advice of the Bishop of Winchester; although it sprung not from the philanthropy, but the policy of Philip: The great and decisive part that she embraced, to prevent his oppression of the Netherlands: All these, together with her successes in Spanish America; She, the champion of the protestants; he, their declared persecutor; no wonder that such a character as Philip hoped, if he could but subdue her, whom he could not deceive, that he should acquire the eternal renown of reuniting the whole Christian world in the catholic communion.

For this purpose, he judged, that to conquer England, would not only be a preparative to re-establish his authority in the Netherlands, but extend his empire, and finally make himself the arbiter of Europe. It lay nearer to Spain than the Netherlands, and was more exposed to invasions from that quarter; after an enemy had once obtained entrance, the difficulty seemed to be over, as it was neither fortified by art nor nature; a long peace had deprived it of *all military discipline and experience;* and the catholics, in which it still abounded, would be ready, it was hoped, to join any invader, who should free them from those persecutions under which they laboured; and would revenge the death of the Queen of Scots, on whom they had fixed all their affections.

The fate of England, he conceived, *must be decided in one battle at* SEA, *and another at* LAND; and what comparison between the English and Spaniards, either in point of naval force, or in the numbers, reputation, and veteran bravery of their armies? For Spain was, at that time, rich and populous;

pulous; he had lately annexed the kingdom of Portugal to his dominions; which, besides securing internal tranquility, had made him master of many settlements in the East Indies, and of the whole commerce of those regions; and had much increased his naval power, in which he was before chiefly deficient.

All the princes of Italy, even the Pope and the court of Rome, were reduced to a kind of subjection under him, and seemed to possess their sovereignty on terms somewhat precarious. The Austrian branch in Germany, with their dependent principalities, was closely connected with him, and was ready to supply him with troops for every enterprize.

All the treasures of the West Indies were in his possession; and the present scarcity of the precious metals, in every country of Europe, rendered the influence of his riches the more forcible and extensive.

Even France, which was wont to counterbalance the Austrian greatness, had lost all her force from intestine commotions; and, as the catholics, the ruling party, were closely connected with Philip, he rather expected thence an augmentation than a diminution of his power.

Upon the whole, such prepossessions were every where entertained, concerning the force of the Spanish monarchy, that all Europe looked upon the diadem as plucked from the head of Elizabeth, when Philip's intentions were known; and England as totally overwhelmed and completely subdued, by his vast resources, his all-commanding influence, and his great military force.

Elizabeth, who was rather cautious than enterprizing in her natural temper, ever needed more to be impelled

by

by the vigour, than reftrained by the prudence of her minifters. But when fhe faw an evident neceffity, fhe braved danger with magnanimous courage; and, trufting to her own confummate wifdom, and to the affections of her people, however divided by religion, fhe prepared herfelf to refift, and even to affault, the whole force of the catholic monarch.

THREE whole years had been fpent by Philip, in fecretly making great preparations, for this diftinguifhed enterprize. This project, indeed, was formed after the Queen of Scots had been perfuaded to make over to him her right to England, as being the only plan to reftore there the catholic religion. Befides this vague right, conveyed by will, he thought he might juftly claim the crown of England, as being the next catholic prince, defcended by the female line, from the Duke of Lancafter, fourth fon to Edward III. and he determined to proceed immediately to the execution of his ambitious project.

POPE Sextus IV. not lefs ambitious than Philip, excited him to the Invafion of England. He again excommunicated the queen, and publifhed a crufade againft her, with the ufual indulgences. All the ports of Spain refounded with preparations for this alarming expedition; and the Spaniards feemed to threaten the Englifh with a total annihilation.

THE fleet, which, on account of its prodigious ftrength, was called "The Invincible Armada," was compleated in 1588. A confecrated banner was procured from the Pope, and the gold of Peru was lavifhed on the occafion. This tremenduous armament, confifted of the following particulars: 19,290 foldiers; 8,250 feamen; 2,008 galley flaves; and 2,630 pieces of ordnance.

THE

The Marquis of Santa Cruz, an officer of great reputation and experience, was appointed to command the Armada; and, by his councils and directions, all the naval preparations were conducted. There was hardly a noble family in Spain, but sent either a son, a brother, or a nephew, on board this fleet, in order to acquire riches and estates in England, which was considered an easy conquest.

In all the ports of Sicily, Naples, Spain, and Portugal, citizens were employed in building vessels of uncommon size and force; naval stores were bought at a great expence; provisions amassed, armies levied, and quartered in the maritime towns of Spain; and plans laid for fitting out such a fleet and embarkation, as had never before had its equal in Europe.

The military preparations in Flanders, were no less formidable. Troops, from all quarters, were every moment assembling, to reinforce the Duke of Parma. Capizuchi and Spinelli, conducted forces from Italy. The Marquis of Borgant, a prince of the house of Austria, levied troops in Germany. The Walloons and Burgundian regiments were compleated or augmented. The Spanish infantry was supplied with recruits; and an army of 34,000 men was assembled in the Netherlands, and kept in readiness to be transported into England. The Duke of Parma employed all the carpenters whom he could procure, either in Flanders or in Lower Germany, and the coasts of the Baltic; and he built at Dunkirk, and Newport, but especially at Antwerp, a great number of boats and flat bottomed vessels, for the transporting of his infantry and cavalry.

The most renowned nobility and princes of Italy and Spain, were ambitious of sharing in the honour of this great enterprize. Don Amadæus of Savoy, Don John of Medicis,

Vespasian

Vespasian Gonzaga, Duke of Sabionetta, and the Duke of Pastrana, hastened to join the army under the Duke of Parma. About 2000 volunteers in Spain, many of them men of family, had enlisted in the service; and no doubts were entertained but that such vast preparations, conducted by officers of such consummate skill, must finally be succesful.

The English fleet, at this time, consisted only of twenty eight sail, most of which were very small vessels; *but the* ALACRITY *of Elizabeth's subjects, sufficiently atoned for the weakness of her navy. The* MARITIME TOWNS, *the* NOBILITY *and* GENTRY, *testified the greatest zeal on this occasion. The* CITY *of London fitted out* THIRTY *ships, though fifteen only had been required. The* GENTRY *and* NOBILITY *hired and armed* FORTY-THREE *ships, at their own expence.*

Lord Howard, of Effingham, a man of great courage and capacity, was lord admiral, and took upon him the command of the navy. Drake, Hawkins, and Forbisher, the most renowned seamen in Europe, served under him. The main fleet was stationed at Plymouth; while a smaller fleet, consisting of forty vessels, under the command of Lord Seymour, lay off Dunkirk, in order to intercept the forces commanded by the Duke of Parma.

Twenty thousand LAND FORCES *were cantoned along the Southern coasts of England; another body of* DISCIPLINED TROOPS *encamped at Tilbury,* near the mouth of the Thames, under the command of the Earl of Leicester; whom the queen, on this occasion, created general in chief of all her forces; and the lord of Hunsdon *commanded a* THIRD ARMY, *consisting of* THIRTY THOUSAND MEN, *for the defence of her majesty's person; and to march to that part of the coast on which the enemy might make their* CHIEF LANDING.

ARTHUR

ARTHUR Lord Grey, Sir Francis Knowles, Sir John Norreys, Sir Richard Bingham, and Sir Roger Williams, men renowned for their valour and experience, *were consulted about the management of the war; and, pursuant to their advice,* ALL THE LANDING PLACES *on the coast, from* HULL *to the* LAND'S-END, *and thence to* MILFORD-HAVEN, *were* FORTIFIED *and* GARRISONED.

The MILITIA *of the country were* ARMED *and* REGULATED *under* PROPER OFFICERS, *who received instructions for* INTERRUPTING *the* DISEMBARKATION *of the* ENEMY; WASTING *the country before them,* ATTACKING *their* REAR, *and keeping up a* CONTINUAL ALARM *in their* ARMY, *till a sufficient force could be assembled* TO GIVE THEM BATTLE.

SIR Robert Sydney was sent into Scotland, in order to induce James, the reigning monarch of that kingdom, to continue firmly attached to the English interest. The Scotish monarch was sufficiently disposed to cultivate an union with Elizabeth, and even to march at the head of all the forces in his kingdom, to the assistance of the English.

HER authority with the King of Denmark, and the connection resulting from their common religion, prevailed upon that prince to seize a squadron of ships, which Philip had either purchased or hired in the Danish harbours.— These were her great allies.

But her chief hopes of success, were placed on THE AFFECTIONS OF HER PEOPLE!

THE very papists themselves, though they knew the Pope had absolved them from their oaths of allegiance, exerted themselves on this occasion. Conscious that they could not expect to be intrusted with authority, *several of the*

the young catholic nobility ſerved as volunteers, either in the fleet or army; ſome equipped ſhips at their own expence, and gave the command of them to proteſtants; while others were active in animating their tenants and vaſſals, in ſupport of their Sovereign. PARTY DISTINCTIONS WERE FORGOT‑TEN, AND EVERY MAN EXERTED HIMSELF IN THE DE‑FENCE OF HIS COUNTRY.

THE magnanimity of Elizabeth was remarkable on this trying occaſion. She appeared on horſeback, in the camp of *Tilbury;* harangued her army, and expreſſed an entire confidence in their loyalty and courage, in ſuch *forcible eloquence* of PATRIOT VIRTUE, that, while we read her oration with rapture, it muſt add a glow to the boſom of every *real friend* to THE CONSTITUTION, when it is conſidered, that it conveys the *ſentiments* of our preſent MOST GRACIOUS MONARCH, to a FREE PEOPLE; not more *loyal*, than HE is *affectionate!*

SPEECH OF ELIZABETH, IN THE CAMP OF TILBURY.

" MY loving people, we have been perſuaded, by ſome
" that are careful of our ſafety, *to take heed how we*
" *commit ourſelves to armed multitudes, for fear of trea-*
" *chery;* but *I aſſure you, I do not deſire to live to diſtruſt*
" *my faithful and loving people.* Let TYRANTS *fear:*
" I have always ſo behaved myſelf, that, *under God, I*
" *have placed my chiefeſt ſtrength and ſafeguard, in the loyal*
" *hearts and good will of my ſubjects.* And therefore I am
" come amongſt you, at this time, not as for my recre-
" ation

" ation or sport, but being resolved, in the midst and
" heat of the battle, to live or die amongst you all; to lay
" down for my God, and for my kingdom, and for my
" people, my honour and my blood, even in the dust.

" I know I have but the body of a weak and feeble wo-
" man; but I have the heart of a king, and of a king of
" England too; and think it foul scorn, that Parma or Spain,
" or any prince of Europe, should dare to invade the borders
" of my realms: To which, rather than any dishonour shall
" grow by me, I myself will take up arms; I myself will
" be your general, judge, and rewarder of every one of
" your virtues in the field.

" I know already, by your forwardness, that you have
" deserved rewards and crowns; and we do assure you, on
" the word of a prince, they shall be duly paid you.

" In the mean time, my lieutenant-general shall be in
" my stead; than whom never prince commanded a more
" noble and worthy subject; not doubting, by your obe-
" dience to my general, by your concord in the camp, and
" your valour in the field, we shall shortly have a famous
" victory over those enemies of my God, of my kingdom,
" and of my people."

The Armada was some time prevented from sailing, by the death of the Marquis of Santa Cruz. The Duke of Madeira Sidonia, a nobleman of great family, but wholely unacquainted with maritime affairs, was appointed admiral in his room. This interval was employed by Elizabeth, in making new preparations for rendering the design abortive.

At length, the invincible fleet sailed from Lisbon, on the twenty-ninth of May; but being overtaken with a dreadful tempest, it was obliged to put into the Groyne, having received considerable damage.

After a delay of two months, the Armada sailed once more to prosecute the intended enterprze. The fleet consisted of 130 ships, of which near 100 were galleons, and of a greater burthen than had ever before appeared on the coast of England. The Spanish admiral was ordered to sail as near the coast of France as possible, in order to join Prince Parma and avoid meeting the English fleet, which might occasion some delay in the enterprize; for it was never imagined that they could make any effectual opposition.

But an accident induced the Spanish admiral to neglect this prudent advice. He took a fishing-boat in his passage, the master of which informed him, that the English admiral, persuaded that the late storm, which scattered the Armada, had prevented any attempt being made this season, had laid up his ships, and discharged the greater part of his seamen. Deceived by this intelligence, the Spaniard, determined to destroy the English ships, in Plymouth harbour, before he joined the Prince of Parma. He accordingly steered towards that port, hoping to obtain an easy victory.

The Armada was disposed in the form of a half-moon, and stretched to the distance of seven leagues, from the extremity of one division to the other. But this tremendous appearance dismayed not the English; they knew their huge vessels were so ill constructed, and so difficult to be managed, that they would not be able to support themselves against the repeated attacks of ships at a distance. Experience soon convinced them they were not mistaken.

Two

Two of the largest ships in the Spanish fleet, were soon after taken, by Sir Francis Drake; and, while the enemy advanced slowly up the Channel, the English followed their rear, and harrassed them with perpetual skirmishes. The Spaniards now began to abate in their confidence of success; the design of attacking the English navy in Plymouth, was laid aside, and they directed their course towards Calais, in order to join the Prince of Parma.

No sooner was the sailing of the Armada made known in England, *than the nobility and gentry hastened out with their ships from every harbour,* to join the admiral, who soon found his fleet amounted to 140 sail. He still hung upon the rear of the Spaniards, and distressed them with repeated attacks.

At last the Armada came to an anchor before Calais, in expectation of being joined by the Prince of Parma; but, before that general could embark his troops, all hopes of success vanished, by a stratagem of the English admiral.

He filled eight of his smaller ships with combustible materials; and, setting them on fire, sent them, one after another, into the midst of the enemy's fleet. Terrified at this appearance, the Spaniards cut their cables, and betook themselves to flight, in a very precipitate and disorderly manner. In the midst of this confusion, the English fell upon them with such fury, that twelve of their largest ships were taken, and several others were thorougly damaged.

The ambitious Spaniards were now convinced that their scheme was entirely frustrated; and would willingly have abandoned the enterprize, and returned immediately to their ports, could they have done it with safety; but this

this was impossible; the wind was contrary; and the only chance of escaping was that of making a tour of the whole island, and reaching at last the Spanish harbours, by the ocean. But a violent storm soon overtook them, and compleated the destruction of the Invincible Armada; not half the vessels returned to the ports of Spain. It is said by some, that Philip, being informed of those disasters, fell on his knees, to thank heaven that his loss was not greater!

While others assert, and with more probability, considering his cruel, bigotted, and vindictive spirit, and his future attempts to invade England, that being at mass when news was brought him of the defeat, he swore, after it was over, "That he would waste and consume his "crown, even to the value of a candlestick, to which he "pointed upon the altar; either to the utter ruin of "England and Elizabeth, or else that he, and all Spain, "should become her tributaries!"

Of the Armada, there were taken and destroyed in the Channel, 15 ships, and 4,791 men; and on the coast of Ireland, 17 ships, and 5,394 men. In all, 32 ships, and 10,185 men.

The lord high-admiral having entirely cleared the English coast of the Spaniards, returned with his fleet to the Downs, and was received in London with the greatest aclamations of joy. A public thanksgiving was ordered to be observed throughout the whole kingdom, for so singular a deliverance; and the queen herself went to St. Paul's, in great solemnity, to perform the sacred duty. At the same time, eleven standards and colours, taken from the enemy, were hung up in the body of the church, as trophies of so distinguished a victory.

THE writers of that age raise their stile by a very pompous description of the Armada; painting it as the most magnificent that had ever appeared upon the ocean, infusing equal terror and admiration into the minds of all beholders. The lofty masts, the swelling sails, and the towering prows of the Spanish galleons, seem impossible to be justly painted, but by assuming the colours of poetry; and an eloquent historian of Italy, in imitation of Camden, has asserted, " That the Armada, though the ships bore every sail, ad-
" vanced with a slow motion, as if the ocean groaned with
" supporting, and the winds were tired with impelling, so
" enormous a weight."

THE truth, however, is, that the largest of the Spanish vessels would scarcely pass for third rates in the present navy of England; yet were they so ill framed, or so ill governed, that they were quite unwieldy, and could not sail upon a wind, nor tack on occasion, nor be managed in stormy weather by the seamen. Neither the mechanics of ship building, nor the experience of mariners, had attained so great perfection as could serve for the security and government of such bulky vessels; and the English, who had already perceived how unserviceable they commonly were, beheld, without dismay, their tremendous appearance.

BUT the Armada was by no means the largest naval force that had been seen in the Channel, either as to numbers of ships, or numbers of men; and had they got into action, it would not have been the greatest that had ever been fought in those seas. When Philip, King of France, opposed the invasion of Edward III. he assembled a fleet of 400 sail, and manned it with 40,000 men; which Edward in person entirely defeated, off the Flemish coast, with a force very far inferior. Both fleets grappling, they fought as if on land, from eight in the morning, till seven at night, when

230 French

230 French ships were taken, and 30,000 Frenchmen were killed; a greater number of ships and men captured and slain, than composed the whole of the Armada of Philip of Spain.

PHILIP'S OTHER ATTEMPTS AT INVASION.

Although Elizabeth was so fortunate in the destruction of the Armada, she knew the irascible temper of Philip too well, to imagine that he would relinquish for ever all ideas of again invading her dominions; and she took every measure to defeat his designs. His discomfiture had begotten, in the nation, a kind of enthusiastic passion for enterprizes against Spain, which she wisely cherished; and nothing seemed now impossible to be achieved by the valour and fortune of the English. She increased her navy, and encouraged the merchants in building large trading vessels; which, on occasion, could be converted into ships of war; and the extensive territories of Philip were every where harrassed by the fleets and armies of Elizabeth.

Philip, on the other hand, intrigued with the catholics in England, and Ireland, and even with King James's subjects of that religion, in Scotland. These formed new projects to place the crown of England upon the head of some person devoted to the Roman faith, or at least not over-zealous for the religion of the protestants. The English catholic fugitives in the Low Countries, fixed on the Infanta Isabella, daughter of Philip, for their sovereign. So bold and open were they in their designs, that they even published a genealogy of her family, to

shew

shew that, the King of Scotland being a heretic, the crown of England devolved to the Spanish monarch, whence they inferred that he had power to dispose of it in favour of his daughter, Isabella.

This was by no means a bare project of the English catholics. It is certain that Philip himself proposed to pursue every measure with the utmost vigour, that might contribute to place the crown offered by the English fugitives on the head of his daughter.

The fame of his preparations, to enable Isabella to mount the throne of England, were known throughout all Europe, in the year 1595, about seven years after the defeat of the Armada; and produced a rebellion in Ireland, under the Earl of Tyrone, encouraged by promises of succour from Philip; besides a considerable ferment among the catholics in England. But the magnanimity and wisdom of Elizabeth braved every danger. Her vigour, her penetration, her vigilance, and her address, were more than a match for the implacable and bigotted Philip's secret wiles, as well as his open hostility.

It may not be amiss here to relate an anecdote of the queen, as it displays her masculine spirit in a singular point of view. The preceding year, in making a speech to Parliament, in which she mentioned the justice and moderation of her government, expressed the small ambition she had ever entertained of making conquests; displayed the just grounds of her quarrel with the King of Spain; discovered how little she apprehended the power of that monarch, even though he should make a greater effort against her, than that of his Invincible Armada; alluded thus to some *dastards* who had fled up the country, when it was in the Channel.

REMARKABLE

A REMARKABLE PASSAGE IN A SPEECH OF QUEEN ELIZABETH'S TO PARLIAMENT.

"*But I am informed, that, when Philip attempted this last* INVASION, *some upon the sea coast* FORSOOK *their towns,* FLED *up higher into the country, and* LEFT ALL NAKED AND EXPOSED *to his entrance: But I swear unto you, by* GOD, *if I knew those persons, or may know of any that shall do so hereafter, I will make them feel what it is to be so* FEARFUL *in so* URGENT A CAUSE."

THE Spaniards, to favour their new invasion, descended to the most vile artifices. They bribed Elizabeth's physician, a Jew, two Portuguese, and three of her own subjects, to poison or assassinate her; but they were discovered, and executed. They bribed others to set fire to her fleet; but that plot was likewise detected, without her shipping receiving the least damage. In 1595, they made a petty descent on Cornwall, without doing any other mischief than burning a church, and three small fishing towns.

ALL these attempts, however, served only to put Elizabeth on her guard. In the following year, hearing that Philip was making great preparations in his ports, to invade England and Ireland, she fitted out a fleet of 150 sail, on board of which were 7000 troops, and nearly the same number of seamen. This force was intended to destroy his new Armada, in his own ports. It sailed from Plymouth, in the month of June; and, after a desperate action, off Cadiz, which lasted from the dawn of day till noon, the Spaniards resolved to sink their ships, and escape

escape to shore. The admiral's ship, St. Philip, and two others, were burnt by the Spaniards, to prevent their falling into the hands of the English. The St. Matthew and St. Andrew were taken, and most of the others run ashore.

During this battle at sea, Sir Walter Raleigh burnt the merchantmen in Port Real, while the Earl of Essex, commander of the land forces, disembarked with the troops, took and burnt Cadiz, and obtained a vast booty. Philip's loss was estimated at 20,000,000 ducats!

The Spanish monarch, though driven to despair by this defeat, and a new league formed against him by England, France, and the United Provinces; but not being able to bring himself to a resolution of relinquishing his projects, nor of leaving to Elizabeth the satisfaction of enjoying the happy success of her own arms, he resolved to make another effort, not only to be revenged on the queen, but even *for the* CONQUEST *of all* ENGLAND.

Though he had received great damage from the English, at Cadiz, yet as it had fallen only upon one of the places where he had made his preparations, he believed himself still in a condition to pursue his pretensions. He assembled, therefore, all the vessels that remained, and freighted besides a great many foreign ships. By this means he was able to send a formidable fleet to sea, at a time, too, when Elizabeth believed him incapable of any naval exertion.

This fleet sailed from Lisbon, to take on board the land forces at Fariola, and then steered directly for England. But a violent storm arising in the midst of the voyage, several of the ships were lost, and the rest so dispersed, that the fleet was rendered unserviceable for that season.

Philip, in 1597, the year following, resolved to attempt an invasion of Ireland; and another of England, by landing on the Cornish coast; but his fleet, as on the preceding year, was dispersed by a storm; and this restless monarch, dying soon after, England was free from all invasions for many years. As for the insults of the Dutch admiral, Van Tromp, on our coast, during the civil war, they need scarcely be mentioned. But the invasion of De Ruyter, another admiral of the States, though trifling in itself, was nearly proving of as serious consequences to destroy us, in the reign of Charles II. had the French king, as was proposed to him, joined his forces then to the Dutch, as that of the Prince of Orange, in the following reign; contributed to save us from *slavery*, *bigotry*, and *ruin*.

CHAP. VI.

OF THE NAVY, OF THE MILITIA, AND OF THE DUTCH INVASION.

THE Revolution in 1688, forms a new epoch in the British Constitution; and was attended with consequences more advantageous to the people, than barely freeing them from an odious government. By deciding many important questions in favour of liberty, and still more, by establishing a new family on the throne; it gave such an ascendant to the genuine principles of *rational, true, and practicable* FREEDOM, as has put the nature of the Constitution beyond all controversy.

It may justly be affirmed, without any danger of exaggeration, *that we, in this island, have ever since enjoyed the most entire system of* LIBERTY *that ever has been known among mankind.*

BETWEEN the reign of Elizabeth, and the abdication of James II. that bulwark against all Invasion, the Navy, was increased in a very great degree. That princess, very sensible how much the defence of the kingdom depended on its naval power, was desirous to encourage commerce and navigation. In the reign of her sister, Mary, the navy of England was so contemptible, that 10,000l. a year was judged sufficient to answer all its necessary charges. Previous to the time of Elizabeth, it was common to hire a navy from foreign powers, but she considerably improved it; yet, when we reflect that, at her death, she had only increased it to forty-two ships; that the four largest carried but forty guns each; that twenty-three of these ships were below 500 tons burthen; that some of them were fifty, and some even of twenty tons; that none but two of them were of a thousand tons; that all the guns belonging to her fleet, were but 774, and these of small dimensions; that there were not 1,300 vessels belonging to all England; that of these there were not much more than 200 which were above eighty tons; and that the whole number of seamen in England, in the year 1582, were not more than 14,295. When we compare, therefore, the trifling naval power of Elizabeth, with that of James II. who extended the navy so much, that it required 42,000 seamen to man it only; it is apparent, that invasions of England became much more complex and difficult, than when those enterprizes were only opposed by sloops of war, and *small merchantmen*; and when the use of gunpowder was so little attended to, that none was manufactured in England, until her reign; when her quarrel with Philip, obliged her to have it made at home, as she was fearful of not obtaining from abroad, in the hour of her necessity, that indispensible article of modern hostility.

But though the naval force of this country was very inconsiderable, till the reigns of Charles II. and James II. the militia, in the time of Elizabeth, was very formidable in numbers, but their DISCIPLINE and EXPERIENCE *were not proportionate*. In the year 1595, to oppose the meditated invasion of the Spanish monarch, the queen made a distribution of *an hundred and forty thousand men*, besides those which Wales could supply; but notwithstanding this, small bodies from Dunkirk and Newport frequently ran over, and plundered the east coast; *so unfit was the militia, as it was then constituted, for the defence of the kingdom.*

ALFRED

ALFRED the Great, as we have already remarked, was the first monarch who established *a regular* MILITIA, for the defence of England. All the people were armed and registered. He fixed their rotation of duty, leaving always a sufficient number for the cultivation of the ground; and so wise and provident were his plans, that the whole nation appeared as one immense garrison, without tillage being at all neglected. Henry II. one of the most amiable, and greatest princes that ever filled the throne of England, made several improvements in the militia. He ordained, according to *property*, to fix an assize of arms.

EVERY man possessed of a knight's fee, containing some hundred acres, should have for each fee, several possessing many, a coat of mail, a helmet, a shield, and a lance; every layman possessed of goods to the value of sixteen marks, was to be armed in a similar manner; every one that possessed goods to the amount of ten marks, was obliged to have an iron gorget, a cap of iron, and a lance; all burgesses were to have a cap of iron, a lance, and a wambais, or coat quilted with wool, tow, or such like materials. It appears that archery, for which the English were afterwards so renowned, had not, at this time, become very common among them. The spear was the chief weapon employed in battle. But in process of time the sovereign, finding that the extent of property was concealed and evaded to avoid arming, their personal service became changed into pecuniary supplies; and the knights themselves, often entered into engagements with the king, to supply him with a certain number of troops at a fixed price.

LAWS were originally made for the encouragement of arms, and particularly archery, on which the defence of the kingdom was supposed so much to depend, before and since the invention of gunpowder. In the reign of Henry VIII.

every

every man was ordered to have a bow; butts, or marks to shoot at, were ordered to be erected in every parish; every bowyer was ordered, for each bow of yew which he made, to make two of elm or wick, for the service of the common people; and the use of cross bows and hand guns were prohibited. What rendered the English bowmen so formidable, was that they carried halberts with them, by which they were enabled, upon occasion, to engage in close fight with the enemy. Frequent musters were made of the people, even during time of peace; and all men of property were obliged to have a compleat suit of armour. The martial spirit of the English, during that age, rendered this precaution, it was thought, sufficient for the defence of the kingdom; and as the power of the sovereign was then absolute, he could instantly, in case of danger, appoint new officers, levy regiments, and collect a militia as numerous as he pleased.

When no FACTION *prevailed among the people, there was no foreign power that ever thought of invading England.* The City of London alone, in these days, could muster *fifteen thousand* men, though it did not contain a fifth part of the present number of its inhabitants.

In Mary's reign, a law was passed, by which each person, according to his property, should be provided with horses, arms, and furniture to serve in the militia, for the defence of the kingdom. A man of a thousand pounds a year, for instance, was obliged to maintain, at his own charge, six horses fit for demi lances, of which three at least were to be furnished with sufficient harness, steel saddles, and weapons, fit for demi lances; and ten horses fit for light horsemen, with furniture and weapons fit for them: He was obliged to have forty corslets furnished; fifty almain revets, or instead of them, forty coats of plate corslets, or brigandines furnished;

furnished; forty pikes, thirty long bows, thirty sheafs of arrows, thirty steel caps or skulls, twenty black bills or halberts, twenty haquebuts, and twenty morians or sallets. A man possessed of 1000 marks of stock, was rated equal to one of 200l. a year.

In Queen Elizabeth's reign, the lord lieutenants were first appointed to the counties; and in the year 1575, all the militia in the kingdom were computed at 182,929; and all the men fit for service, are said, by some, to amount to 1,172,674.

In the following reign, the number of the militia force was 160,000 men; it was well disciplined. The City of London procured the most expert officers that had served abroad, and who taught the trained bands their exercises in the Artillery Garden. All the counties of England, in emulation of the capital, were fond of shewing a well ordered and well appointed militia. The very boys, at this period, in mimickry of their elders, enlisted themselves voluntarily into companies, elected officers, and practised the discipline, of which the models were every day exposed to their view.

When the democratic parliamentary faction, against Charles I. were on the eve of committing overt acts, they seized the militia, by vote, and appointed it with officers of their own selection.

General Monk, while overwhelming the brutal tyrants that had for so many years oppressed the empire, secretly fixed a close correspondence with the City of London, and established its militia, in hands upon whose fidelity he could rely; and when the moderate party had got the ascendancy in parliament, and a council of state was established previous to the restoration, consisting of men of character and moderation,

moderation, the militia of the whole kingdom was put into such hands as would promote order and settlement.

In the beginning of Charles's reign, the militia was deemed so formidable, that when De Wit, the Dutch pensionary, advised the French king, to invade England, during the first Dutch war, that monarch replied, "That such an attempt would be entirely fruitless, and would tend only to unite the English. In a few days after our landing, added he, there will be 50,000 men at least to oppose us."

THE PRINCIPLES OF TRUE LIBERTY, REQUIRE EVERY ENCOURAGEMENT TO BE GIVEN, TOWARDS THE ESTABLISHMENT OF A GREAT AND WELL DISCIPLINED MILITIA; yet was the first parliament of Charles II. strangely jealous of his strictness, in having it properly trained. The militia afterward fell much to decay during his reign, and that of his brother, James II. partly owing to the above cause; and this created, on the part of these princes, a diffidence of their subjects.

But ever since the revolution, the militia has been very properly completely lodged in the hands of the reigning monarch; and his *present* MAJESTY cannot better shew his *paternal regard* and his *real wishes* to SUPPORT *the* TRUE LIBERTIES *of* HIS FREE PEOPLE, than by *increasing* THE MILITIA, at the present moment, as well CAVALRY as INFANTRY; and taking the utmost pains to have them WELL DISCIPLINED, either to *repel* an INVADING FOE, or to *crush* all DEMOCRATIC INSURRECTION. For when, by this means, HE instructs the PEOPLE, in the *use* of ARMS, and *intrusts* them with COMMAND, for the *protection of all that they hold dear on earth;* it is the surest proof of a PATRIOT KING, who confides the security of their COMMON RIGHTS, to a CORPS *that can never act but in* DEFENCE *of the* LIBERTIES *of the* BRITISH EMPIRE.

DUTCH

DUTCH INVASION.

It was thought necessary, in this place, to give the above slight sketch of the history of the militia, our internal bulwark; for while we have a disciplined and numerous militia, and a superior navy, no enemy can invade us, with the least prospect of success.

Had this been the case, in the commencement of the reign of Charles II. during the Dutch and French wars; had he not been a nigard then about the expences of his navy; had his militia, which was deemed formidable, been properly stationed along that part of the coast most likely to have been invaded; he would not have exposed England to one of the greatest affronts which it has ever received.

Relying too securely on the certainty of an approaching peace, Charles laid up all his great ships of war, except two small squadrons; and left the kingdom almost in the same situation as in times of the most profound tranquility. De Wit, that sagacious and enterprizing minister of the States, having the best intelligence from England, he determined to take advantage of the negligence of the British monarch. He ordered the Dutch admiral, De Ruyter, to sail to the mouth of the Thames. There he dispatched Van Ghent, his vice-admiral, with seventeen of his light ships of war, and a few fire ships; who, sailing up the Medway, soon made himself master of Sheerness, notwithstanding it was bravely defended by Sir Edward Spragge. After Van Ghent had burnt the magazines full of stores, to the amount of 40,000l. he blew up the fortifications.

The City of London was in the utmoſt conſternation. Some ſhips were ſunk, and a large chain thrown acroſs the narrow part of the Medway. But the Dutch, having the advantage of a ſpring tide, and an eaſterly wind, preſſed on, and broke it, and ſailed between the ſunk veſſels. They burnt three large men of war that had been lately taken from them; and were placed to guard the chain, the Matthias, the Unity, and the Charles the Fifth; beſides burning and damaging ſeveral others, and carrying off the hull of the Royal Charles.

They advanced as far as Chatham and Upnor Caſtle, with ſix men of war, and five fire ſhips; where they burnt the Royal Oak, the Royal London, and the Great James, all ſhips of importance. The brave Capt. Douglas, the commander of the Royal Oak, periſhed on board her, in the flames, though he had an eaſy opportunity of eſcaping. To thoſe who preſſed him to come aſhore, he exclaimed, "Never was it known that a Douglas had left "his poſt without orders."

After this the Dutch fell down the Medway; and it was apprehended that they might next tide ſail up the Thames, and deſtroy all the ſhips in the river, as far up as London Bridge. The capital was in great confuſion. Nine ſhips were ſunk at Woolwich, and four at Blackwall. Platforms were raiſed in ſeveral places, and furniſhed with artillery. The trained bands were called out, and every precaution was now taken, to render the attempt of the enemy abortive.

But De Ruyter did not think proper to proceed. The danger, he thought, was too great, and the hopes of ſucceſs too precarious. He left the mouth of the Thames, ſtood to the weſtward, and made an attempt to deſtroy the ſhipping at Portſmouth; but was repulſed with conſiderable loſs.

He

He met with no better fuccefs at Plymouth, although he took fome fhips in Torbay.

He was not, however, intimidated. He returned again to the mouth of the Thames, and advanced as far as Tilbury Fort; but found the Englifh fo well prepared for his reception, that there were no hopes of fuccefs. He next infulted Harwich, and gave chace to a fquadron, commanded by Sir Edward Spragge, who was obliged to retire up the Thames. The whole coaft was in alarm, till the conclufion of the peace, which foon happened; and De Ruyter, had the fatisfaction, for near two months, to ride the undifputed mafter of the ocean; to burn the Englifh fhips in their very harbours, to fill every place with confufion, and ftrike a terror into the capital itfelf.

If the French had thought proper, at this time, to have joined the Dutch fleet, and invaded England, confequences the moft fatal might juftly have been apprehended, from the want of all requifite defence, notwithftanding what Lewis faid, when urged by De Wit, then to invade this country; and at which want of forefight, he muft have afterwards been very much chagrined, when he had ferious thoughts of invading Great Britain.

CHAP. VII.

DUKE OF MONMOUTH'S INVASION.

ENGLAND remained free from all hostile attacks from abroad, that can be termed invasions, from that of De Ruyter's, in the year 1667, to the Duke of Monmouth's unsuccessful attempt in 1685, to obtain the crown, by dethroning his uncle, James II. Although we have passed over the invasions of candidates for the crown, in former ages, by not giving them in detail; yet, as Monmouth's invasion happened of a later date, and preceded that of the Prince of Orange, who compleated the glorious revolution; it may not be amiss, to dwell with some minuteness, on the rash and premature attempt, of that unfortunate nobleman.

THE Duke of Monmouth, was a natural son of Charles II. and possessed all the qualities which could engage the affections of the public; a distinguished valour, a thoughtless generosity, and a graceful person; but his capacity was mean, and his temper pliant. It is needless here, to recapitulate the anecdotes of his life, further than to remark, that he had always entertained hopes of succeeding to the crown, on the death of his father; and that when the king once fell sick, he engaged in a conspiracy with Lord Russel, Lord Grey, Lord Shaftesbury, Algernon Sydney and others, that if the sickness proved mortal, to rise in arms, and oppose the Duke of York's succession. But the plot being detected, Russel, Sydney, and others, were executed, and Monmouth pardoned.

A MORTAL

A MORTAL antipathy subsisted between him and his uncle, by whose advice he was banished the kingdom, two years before the death of the king. During that period, he remained at the court of the Prince of Orange, who shewed him all marks of honour and distinction. But when James ascended the throne, the prince thought it politic, to dismiss Monmouth and all his followers. He was then induced to make a landing in England, though the nation was not then ripe for a revolt. For the grievances of that reign, were hitherto of small importance: and the people were not as yet, in a disposition to remark them with great severity.

THE Duke sailed from the Texel, in a ship of thirty guns, accompanied with two other vessels. There were on board, several English exiles from Flanders, *men of desperate fortunes, and who had no means of retrieving their affairs but by a* CHANGE *of* GOVERNMENT *at home*.

THEY met with such contrary winds, that they were nineteen days at sea, and landed on the 8th of June, at Lime, in Dorsetshire. Though he had scarcely a hundred followers at landing, so popular was his name, that in four days, he had assembled above 2000 horse and foot. They were, indeed, almost all of them the lowest of the people; and the declaration which he published, was chiefly calculated to suit the prejudices of the vulgar, or the most bigotted of the whig party.

MONMOUTH, though he had formerly given many proofs of personal courage, had not the vigour of mind requisite for such a great undertaking. After marching through many towns in the west, and proclaiming himself in all these places, he attacked the king's army at Sedgemoor, near Bridgewater; where, after a desperate combat of three hours, he was totally vanquished. He fled from the field
of

of battle, above twenty miles, till his horse sunk under him. He then changed clothes with a peasant, in order to conceal himself. The peasant was discovered by the pursuers, who now redoubled the diligence of their search; at last he was found in a ditch, covered with fern, quite spent with fatigue, and some green pease in his pocket, the only food he had eaten since his defeat.

When he arrived in London, after he had a fruitless interview with the king, he was ordered for immediate execution. He was brought to the scaffold, on the 15th of July, and met his death in a manner that became his rank and character. He warned the executioner not to fall into the error which he had committed, in beheading Lord Russel; where he was obliged to redouble the blow. But this precaution had not the desired effect, for it so intimidated the man, that he could strike only a feeble blow on the neck of Monmouth; who raised his head from the block, and looked him in the face, as if reproaching him for his failure. He again laid down his head, and the executioner struck him twice, but without effect; on which he threw aside the axe, and declared himself incapable of finishing the bloody office. The sheriff, however, obliged him to renew the attempt, and at two blows more, the head was severed from the body.

Thus died, in the thirty-sixth year of his age, James, Duke of Monmouth, whose character, in many respects, was truly amiable. He was the darling of the people; the consciousness of which, and the allurement of ambition, had engaged him in enterprizes far beyond his capacity; and which, in the end, cost him his life.

CHAP.

CHAP. VIII.

INVASION OF THE PRINCE OF ORANGE, AND THE ESTABLISHMENT OF THE REVOLUTION.

THIS victory of King James, over a formidable rival, in the commencement of his reign, had it been managed with prudence, would naturally have tended much to increase his power and authority. But by reason of the cruelty with which it was prosecuted in the west, by Lord Chief-Justice Jefferies and Colonel Kirke, with the connivance of the king, and of the temerity with which it afterwards inspired him; it was a principal cause of his sudden ruin and downfall.

WHEN the nation, by repeated flagrant acts of the sovereign, were fully convinced that he was absolutely determined to subvert the Constitution, both in church and state; they thought it full time to form a scheme for preventing the destruction of their laws, religion, and liberties.

THE Prince of Orange, nephew to the king by birth, and his son-in-law by marrying Lady Mary, his daughter, was fixed upon for their deliverer. All persons, though of opposite parties, whigs, tories, churchmen, and nonconformists,

conformists, formed an union, and concurred in their applications to that prince. And thus all faction was, for a time, laid asleep in England; and rival parties, forgetting their animosity, had secretly concurred in a design of resisting their rash, inflexible, and misguided monarch.

Their solicitations to the prince were not in vain. He was easily engaged to yield to them, and to embrace the defence of a nation, which, during its present fears and distresses, regarded him as its sole protector. He was peculiarly happy, throughout his whole life, in the situations in which he was placed. Silent and thoughtful; given to hear and to enquire; of a sound and steady understanding; firm in what he once resolved, or once denied; strongly intent on business, little on pleasure: By these virtues he engaged the attention of all men. He saved his own country from ruin. He restored the liberties of Britain. He supported the general independency of Europe. And thus, though his virtue, it is confessed, is not the purest which we meet with in history; it will be difficult to find any person, whose actions and conduct have contributed more eminently to the general interests of society and of mankind.

When the prince had determined to put himself at the head of the protestant party in England, he desired several of the nobility, who waited on him at the Hague, to demand the assistance of the States, in the name of the whole kingdom, which they easily obtained.

When King James heard of the Prince of Orange's designs and preparations for an invasion, he became distracted with fears and apprehensions. Having received certain advice that he might soon expect to see the Dutch fleet upon the coast, with a land army on board, accompanied with many English noblemen and persons of distinction,

tinction, who had, for some time, concealed themselves in Holland; he was so terrified, that neither he nor his council could form any plausible scheme for opposing their invasion. In this alarming exigency, he adopted some popular measures, which failed of producing the desired effect: They came too late, and were generally considered as the result of fear, rather than that of inclination, or a real change of sentiment.

During these transactions, the Prince applied himself with the greatest assiduity to complete his armament; and, as soon as every thing was finished, he published a manifesto, explaining the true motives for his expedition. He solemnly disclaimed in it, all thoughts of conquest; declaring that his sole intention was that of maintaining the protestant religion, and the laws and liberties of these kingdoms, which had been so openly violated; and the procuring a free parliament, which might, at once, settle all the rights of the subject, and the prerogatives of the crown, on a firm basis; and that he had no idea of disturbing his father-in-law in the enjoyment of the sovereignty. He added, that he had undertaken this necessary and difficult task, at the invitation of many lords, both ecclesiastical and civil; by numbers of gentlemen, and other subjects in these realms, of all ranks.

The prince's measures were all so well concerted, that, in three days, above 400 transports were hired; and the army being embarked, quickly fell down the rivers and canals from Nimeguen. The artillery, arms, stores, and horses, were embarked; and the prince sailed from Helvoet Sluys, with a fleet of near 500 vessels, and an army of 14,000 men. After sailing about fourteen leagues, the wind shifted to the west, and blew so violent a storm, that in a very few hours, scarce three ships were to be seen together.

But this loss being soon repaired, the fleet put again to sea, under the command of Admiral Herbert, and stood away, with a fair wind, towards the west of England. The same wind which favoured the Dutch, detained the king's fleet in the river; and gave the prince an opportunity of passing the Streights of Dover, without molestation. Both shores were covered with multitudes of people, who, besides admiring the grandeur of the spectacle, were held in anxious suspence, at the prospect of an enterprize the most important that had, for some years, been undertaken in this part of the world.

After a prosperous voyage, the prince landed his army safely in Torbay, on the 5th of November, the anniversary of the gunpowder treason. The Dutch army marched immediately to Exeter, and there the prince's declaration was published. But the whole country was so terrified at the dreadful executions that had ensued on Monmouth's invasion, that nobody, for several days, joined the prince. The Bishop of Exeter fled with the utmost precipitation to London, and carried to court the first intelligence of this invasion. The king was so pleased with this instance of zeal, that he rewarded the prelate with the Archbishopric of York, which had been long kept vacant, with an intention of bestowing it on some catholic.

Major Barrington was the first person who joined the prince, and his example was soon followed by the gentry of the counties of Devon and Somerset.

By degrees, the whole kingdom was in commotion. But the most alarming symptom was the disaffection, which, from the general spirit of the people, not from any particular reason, had crept into the army. The officers all seemed to prefer the interest of their country, and of their religion, before those principles of honour and fidelity

fidelity which are esteemed the most sacred ties by men of that profession.

Several officers of distinction informed Feversham, their general, that they could not, in conscience, fight against the Prince of Orange, who came to defend the protestant cause; and many deserted the king; among the rest, Lord Churchill, afterwards Duke of Marlborough.

Distracted and perplexed at such alarming circumstances, James suddenly took the resolution of returning to London, from Salisbury, where he had marched to oppose the prince; a measure which could have no other tendency than that of betraying his fears, and provoking farther treachery, which soon happened. Churchill and his lady had acquired an absolute ascendance over the family of Prince George of Denmark; and a seasonable opportunity now offered, for overwhelming the unhappy king, who was staggering under the violent shocks he had received from his adverse fortune.

The first stage of his majesty's retreat, towards London, was Andover; and there Prince George, with the young Duke of Ormond, Sir George Hu..., and several other persons of distinction, deserted him in the night, and retired to the camp of the Prince of Orange. As soon as the news reached London, the Princess of Denmark, afterwards Queen Anne, pretended to dread the king's displeasure, and withdrew herself, in company with the Bishop of London, and Lady Churchill. She fled to Nottingham, where the Earl of Dorset received her with the greatest respect; and the gentry of the county soon formed a troop for her protection.

The wretched king was no ways prepared for this astonishing event. He burst into tears, when the first intelligence

telligence was conveyed to him. In this incident, he doubtless foresaw the total expiration of his royal authority. But the nearer and more intimate concern of a parent, seized his heart, when he found himself abandoned by a virtuous child, whom he had always regarded with the most tender affection. "God help me!" cried he, in the extremity of his agony, "my own children "have forsaken me!"

It is indeed singular, that a prince, whose chief blame consisted in imprudencies and misguided principles, should be exposed from religious antipathy, to such treatment as even Nero, Domitian, or the most enormous tyrants that have disgraced the records of history, never met with from their friends and family.

The Prince of Orange, having received advice of the king's return to London, advanced with his army to Sherborne, and thence to Salisbury, which he entered in triumph; the king's forces having some days before retired to Reading.

The king, finding himself attacked and pursued by one of his sons-in-law; abandoned by the other; like another Lear, deserted by his own daughters; betrayed by his bosom friends; and abandoned by his subjects; he considered his fortune as desperate.

He was alarmed every moment with new proofs of the revolt. Therefore not daring to repose confidence in any but those equally exposed to danger with himself; agitated by indignation, at the ingratitude of some; by despair, at the infidelity of others; impelled by fears for his own and his adherents safety; he precipitately embraced the resolution of withdrawing to France; and accordingly sent off before hand, the queen and the infant prince, under the

conduct

conduct of Count Lauzun, an old favourite of the French Monarch. He himself disappeared in the night, attended only by Sir Edward Hales, a new convert, and made the best of his way to a ship, which waited for him near the mouth of the river.

The king left a letter for his general, the Earl of Feversham, in which he declared, that if he could have relied upon all his troops, he should not have been driven to this extremity; without hazarding one battle, in support of his crown and dignity. But as the whole army seemed disposed to desert him, he thought it madness to venture himself at their head, against the Prince of Orange. He thanked the general and all the officers that had been faithful to him; desired them not to risque their lives and fortunes, by an unavailing opposition; but at the same time cautioned them not to enter into any association against his interest.

Language cannot describe the surprize that seized the city, the court, and the nation, at the king's flight; and the more to increase the confusion which James knew must be the natural consequence of his taking such a step; he did not name any person who should, in his absence, conduct the affairs of the public. He threw the great seal into the river; burnt all the writs which had been made out for electing a new parliament; and caused a caveat to be entered against those which were actually issued.

As soon as the general was informed of his majesty's retreat, he disbanded the troops which were in the neighbourhood of London; and, without either paying or disarming them, left them to plunder the country at pleasure.

The Prince of Orange, in the interim, arrived at Windsor, in his way to London, to settle the affairs of the nation with the lords, by whom he was expected, on the supposition,

fition, that the king was fled over to the Continent, and had totally refigned the reins of government. But, to the no fmall furprize of the prince, news fuddenly arrived, that his majefty had been difcovered at Feverfham, in Kent, where he was waiting for a veffel to carry him to France; and after fuffering many fevere indignities from the populace; who, not knowing his perfon, had miftaken him for fome catholic of quality, endeavouring to make his efcape from the country, whereupon they confined him. The peers, hearing that his majefty was ftill in his own dominions, fent down the Earls of Middleton, Aylefbury, Yarmouth, and Feverfham, with a detachment of the guards to attend the king to London, whither he immediately returned. The populace, touched with compaffion for his unhappy fate, received him with fhouts and acclamations of joy. An exprefs was immediately difpatched to the prince of Orange, acquainting him with the return of his majefty to London.

Nothing feemed more wanting in this alarming crifis, on the fide of the victorious party, than how to difpofe of the king's perfon. For though the prince may be juftly fuppofed to have poffeffed more humanity and generofity to an unhappy monarch, fo nearly related to him, yet he alfo knew that nothing would fo effectually promote his own views, as the retreat of James into France; a country, at all times, fufficiently obnoxious to the Englifh. It was, therefore, determined to pufh him into that meafure, which he himfelf feemed very ready to adopt.

The king fent Lord Feverfham on a civil meffage, defiring a conference with the prince, in order to quiet the nation; but that nobleman was put under an arreft, on pretence of his wanting a paffport. The Dutch guards were ordered to take poffeffion of Whitehall, where the king then lodged, and difplaced the Englifh; while a meffage was carried to him after midnight, ordering him to repair to Ham, near Richmond.

Richmond. He defired permiffion to go to Rochefter, which was granted.

This fufficiently proved that the artifice had taken effect; and that the king, terrified with this harfh treatment, had renewed his former refolution of leaving the kingdom.

James, although he did not intend to return to Whitehall, thought proper to continue fome days at Rochefter, under the protection of a Dutch guard, hoping he might yet receive an invitation to keep poffeffion of the throne. But obferving the church, the nobility, the city, the country, had all concurred in neglecting him, and leaving him to follow his own counfels, he fubmitted to his melancholy fate; and being urged by earneft letters from the queen, he privately embarked on board a frigate, which waited for him, and arrived fafely at Ambleteufe, in Picardy, on the 23d of December.

Thus was the invafion of the Prince of Orange eafily achieved; and thus ended the reign of a prince, whom, if we confider his perfonal character, rather than his public conduct, we may fafely pronounce him more unfortunate than criminal. He had many of thofe qualities which form a good citizen: Even fome of thofe, which, had they not been fwallowed up in bigotry and arbitrary principles, ferve to compofe a good fovereign. In domeftic life, his conduct was irreproachable, and is entitled to our approbation. Severe, but open in his enmities; fteady in his councils; diligent in his fchemes; brave in his enterprizes; faithful, fincere, and honourable in his dealings with all men.

Such was the character with which the Duke of York mounted the throne of England. In that high ftation, his frugality of public money was remarkable; his induftry exemplary;

exemplary; his application to naval affairs fuccefsful; his encouragement of trade judicious; his jealoufy of national honour laudable: What then was wanting to make him an excellent monarch? That to which our AMIABLE SOVEREIGN is fo *particularly devoted;* a peculiar *regard* and *affection* to the RELIGION and the CONSTITUTION *of his country.* Had James been poffeffed of this effential quality, aided by fo many virtues, he would have rendered his reign honourable and happy. When it was wanting, every excellence, which he poffeffed, became dangerous and pernicious to his kingdom; but which, in the end, produced the GLORIOUS REVOLUTION; a Revolution conducted with fuch *prudence,* and formed of fuch *pre-eminent materials,* of THAT THEORY which was REALLY PRACTICABLE; that it *fixed* the CONSTITUTION of GREAT BRITAIN on the moft *folid bafis* that had been ever yet known in the univerfe, for the TRUE HAPPINESS OF MAN.

CHAP. IX.

INVASION OF IRELAND, BY JAMES, AND ATTEMPT AT AN INVASION OF ENGLAND, IN HIS FAVOUR, BY LEWIS XIV.

THE impolitic and inconfiderate management of Charles II. and James II. as to the friendly correfpondence held between them and the French king, manifeftly appeared by the prodigious growth of his naval power. France was fo weak in this refpect, under the adminiftration of the great Cardinal Richelieu, that this high-fpirited minifter was forced, in very preffing terms, to folicit affiftance from Sweden; and even fo late as Cromwell's ufurpation, in the beginning of the reign of Lewis XIV. he fhewed the utmoft contempt for the French power at fea.

It was our wars with the Dutch, in the reign of Charles II. that gave the French, as they themfelves confefs, firft an opportunity of learning, at the expence of the maritime powers, what it was to make a figure on an element, with which, before, they were but little acquainted. This knowledge they fo far artfully improved, by fometimes fiding with the Dutch, and fometimes with us, that in the fpace of lefs than twenty years, they found themfelves able to cope with either nation; and, in 1676, actually beat the united

united Dutch and Spanish fleets, in the Mediterranean, and killed the famous Admiral De Ruyter.

At the Revolution, the French were grown so strong, that they were able to dispute the empire of the ocean, against the joint forces of both the maritime powers; so that although Charles and James took great pains to increase and discipline their navy, yet, by their want of policy in respect to that of France, the navy of England, in point of comparative strength with the other, was far inferior to what it was at the time of Cromwell, however much it had since then increased in numbers, power, and skill.

Some years before the Revolution, the French fleet consisted of upwards of 200 sail; carrying 7,080 pieces of cannon, and 39,477 men; and the English fleet at the Revolution, was composed of but 173 vessels, carrying 6,930 pieces of cannon, and having on board 42,003 men.

It is necessary to mention these facts, to shew that the fleets of both countries, were nearly upon an equality, when William and Mary mounted the English throne.

James had not been many months in France, when Lewis ordered 5000 troops to favour the abdicated monarch's invasion of Ireland, as a preparatory step to his regaining the British crown. This force was embarked in a fleet of fourteen ships of the line, seven frigates, three fire ships, with a great number of transports. They sailed from Brest, on the 17th of March, and on the 22d of the same month, landed safely at Kinsale, in Ireland. It is not consistent with the plan of this work, to dwell on the Irish invasion, further than to remark, that King William, in the end, totally defeated the forces under James, and obliged him again to take refuge in France. William appeared so superior

rior at the decisive battle of the Boyne, that the Irish said, "If the English would change king's with them, they would fight the battle over again."

But while William was in Ireland, and the government of England left in the hands of his royal consort, Queen Mary, the utmost vigilance was required to prevent the ruin of the nation, from the intrigues of James's abettors, since stiled Jacobites. But the queen sustained the weight of affairs with great prudence. In the absence of the king, the Jacobites were concerting measures with France, to put their designs in execution, of restoring James to the throne. An Invasion of England, by France, was completely settled. It was agreed, that part of the French fleet should bear up the Thames, to countenance the Jacobites in London, who were grown very bold and numerous, by the flocking thither of a great number of that party, from all parts of the country; and that they should raise an insurrection, and seize the queen and her chief ministers.

This being effected, certain persons were to have taken upon them the administration of affairs, till the return of King James, who was to leave his command of the army in Ireland, to his generals, and hasten with all speed, to England. The other part of the French fleet having joined their gallies, was to have landed 8000 men at Torbay, with arms for a greater number; after which the gallies and men of war were to sail to the Irish seas, and hinder the return of William and his forces; and the discontented Scots were to have revolted, at the same time, in several parts of that kingdom.

The French fleet entered the Channel as before concerted; at a moment, too, when the English were ill prepared to receive them; occasioned by an impolitic compliment, paid by King William to the new married Spanish queen, in escorting

escorting her with an English fleet, from Holland to the Groyne. Admiral Ruffel was ordered to attend her, with a squadron, which was partly to confist of some belonging to a fleet that was going to the Mediterranean, under Admiral Killegrew, to watch the motions of the French in their preparations at Toulon. The Admiral was so long delayed by contrary winds, that he did not return from the Groyne till the latter end of April, when the squadron put into Plymouth to refit, and he went to Spithead. By this means, a design of blocking up Toulon, was not only lost, as the French failed before the English arrived there, but the squadron at Plymouth, joined by that which came from the Irish seas, in all 30 ships of the line, were prevented from joining the grand fleet at Spithead, by the French entering the Channel, while they lay thus divided.

It was also said, that the commander in chief, Lord Torrington, was dilatory in forming a junction, owing to his not believing that the French were in such forwardness. So trifling indeed, were his apprehensions of their arrival, that he had neglected to appoint sloops of observation to cruize to the westward, in order to watch their motions. They sailed with so fair a wind, that they were off the Isle of Wight before he had notice of their being in the Channel; and in all probability, they would have surprized him, had not the wind suddenly shifted.

Another reason alledged for the fleet lying so long at Spithead, was, their expectation of being joined by a squadron of the Dutch.

Lord Torrington was at St. Helen's when he received the news from Weymouth, that the French fleet from Brest, confisting of 78 ships, and 22 fire ships, had entered the Channel. Having been joined by the Dutch fleet, though the Plymouth squadron was prevented joining him, by contrary

trary winds, it seemed to be the opinion of a council of war, that it would be imprudent to meet the enemy, as the whole combined fleet did not exceed fifty-six sail; but before any resolution was taken, an express arrived from the queen, with positive orders to hazard an engagement at all events, rather than suffer the enemy to sail up the Channel, and insult the English coast and harbours.

In obedience to this order, as soon as it was light, on the 30th of June, the admiral threw out the signal for drawing into a line, and bore down upon the enemy, while they were under sail, by a wind, with their heads to northward. The signal for battle was made about eight, when the French braced their head-sails to their masts, in order to lie by.

The action began about nine, when the Dutch squadron, which made the van of the united fleets, fell in with the van of the French, and put them into some disorder. About half an hour thereafter, our blue squadron engaged their rear very warmly; but the red, commanded by the Earl of Torrington in person, which made the center of the English fleet, could not come up till about ten; and this occasioned a great opening between them and the Dutch.

The French, making use of this advantage, weathered, and of course surrounded the latter, who defended themselves very gallantly, though they suffered extremely from so unequal a force. The admiral, seeing their distress, endeavoured to relieve them; and while they dropped their anchors, the only method they had to preserve themselves, he drove with his own ship and several others, between them and the enemy, and in that situation anchored about five in the afternoon, when it grew calm; but discerning how much the Dutch had suffered, and how little proba-

bility

bility there was of regaining any thing, by renewing the fight, he weighed about nine at night, and retired eastward with the tide of flood.

A MANŒUVRE of the Dutch admiral, who ordered his ships to drop their anchors, with their sails standing, saved his squadron. The tide set strongly up the Channel; and there being very little wind, the French, who were ignorant of the stratagem, were soon hurried away by the tide, while the Dutch continued safe at anchor, beyond the reach of their cannon. They had, however, received considerable damage; their two vice-admirals were killed, and several of their ships so greatly shattered, that they were obliged to sink them, in order to prevent their falling into the hands of the enemy.

THE next day, it was resolved to preserve the fleet, by retreating; and rather to destroy the disabled ships, if they should be pressed by the enemy, than to hazard another engagement, by endeavouring to protect them. This resolution was executed with great success, which, however, was owing to want of experience in the French admirals; for by not anchoring when the English did, they were driven to a great distance; and, by continuing to chace in a line of battle, instead of leaving every ship to do her utmost, they could never recover what they lost by their first mistake.

BUT notwithstanding all this, they pressed on their pursuit as far as Rye-bay, and forcing one of our men of war of 70 guns, called the Anne, which had lost all her masts, on shore, near Winchelsea; they sent in two ships to burn her, which the captain prevented, by setting fire to her himself. The body of the French fleet stood in and out of the Bays of Bourne and Pensey, in Sussex, while about fourteen of their ships anchored near the shore.

THE

The English lost, in this unfortunate affair, only two ships, two of their captains, and about 400 men. But the nation was exasperated, to the highest pitch, at the improvident conduct of Lord Torrington; and they were justly alarmed at this disaster, so trivial in itself, but which appeared so fatal in its consequences to the protestant interest, and consequently to the liberties of Britain. It was the common opinion, that if the English admiral had followed the example of the Blue Squadron, and brought on a close engagement, that the enemy must have been totally defeated; which, in all probability, would have been fatal to the French, as it was almost impossible for the remnant of the vanquished fleet to have returned to Brest, without being captured or destroyed by the squadron then lying ready in Plymouth Sound. The conduct of Torrington was censured by his own admirals; and he was sent to the Tower, on his arrival in London; but after being confined there for some time, and brought to trial, he was acquitted; not without great murmurs, at the partiality with which that trial was said to have been conducted.

If we consider, however, this victory of the French impartially, and the defence which the English admiral made; that the preparations for the fleet were very late; that it was much inferior to the enemy, and badly manned; that he laboured under great want of intelligence; and that consequently the orders he had received for fighting, was against his judgment, and that of the council of war; the admiral may be acquitted, as to any sinister design, though he cannot as to prudential foresight and indefatigable diligence. The combined fleets carried, at the utmost, but about 3,462 guns; whereas, that of France carried 4,702, besides being much better manned.

Our fleet, after the engagement, retreated towards the Thames, and the admiral went on shore. He left orders

to

to anchor above the Middle Grounds; and to appoint two frigates to ride, one at the buoy of the Spits, the other at the lower end of the Middle; and to take away the buoys, and immediately retreat, if the enemy approached. But, should the French press the English fleet further, the commander was ordered, in like manner, to take away the buoys near him, and to attack him with his fire ships; still, however, retiring, and making the proper signals in such cases.

On the 8th of July, the enemy steered to the coast of France, but returned again, and were seen off the Berry Head, a little to the eastward of Dartmouth; where, the wind shifting, they put into Torbay. There they lay not long; for they were discovered on the 29th, near Plymouth, at which place the necessary preparations were made by platforms, and other works, to give them a warm reception. They appeared again, off the Ram Head, on the 5th of August, to the number of near seventy ships; when, standing westward, they were no more seen this year in the Channel.

It was deemed surprising, that the French should hover so long, and so quietly, on the coast of England, without making any further attempts; but they were still in expectation, as it afterwards appeared, *of the effects of a conspiracy of the Jacobites, which was planned to commence on the 18th of June.* But they excused themselves, *owing to their* LEADERS *being mostly* SEIZED. In all this time, the French were masters of the sea, and our coasts open to them. Had they followed the first panic, they might have done considerable mischief, as there were not then in England above SEVEN THOUSAND SOLDIERS. The Militia was raised; and, though the harvest approached, which rendered it inconvenient for many to be absent from their labour, yet the nation shewed so much zeal and affection to their majesties,

and

and the glorious Constitution, which had been so recently established; that the Jacobites, all over England, durst not appear, for fear of being insulted by the populace.

INDEED the retreat of Lord Torrington had no sooner reached the capital, than the fears of an invasion created a general consternation, which immediately spread through the whole kingdom. The queen took every step to inspire her subjects with resolution. THE CITY OF LONDON, AT THIS MOMENT, STOOD PRE-EMINENTLY FORWARD. The lord mayor and aldermen, attended her majesty in council, and declared the unanimous resolution of the city to preserve THEIR MAJESTIES and THE CONSTITUTION, to the utmost of their power, and with the hazard of their lives. They represented that the several regiments of the city, consisting of about NINE THOUSAND MEN, *were complete, well armed, well appointed, and ready immediately, to proceed in* THEIR MAJESTIES' SERVICE. That the *lieutenancy* also had resolved, *that six regiments of auxiliaries should be raised for the service; and that the* LORD MAYOR, ALDERMEN, *and* COMMON COUNCIL *would, by the* VOLUNTARY CONTRIBUTION *of* THEMSELVES *and* OTHER CITIZENS, forthwith raise A LARGE REGIMENT OF HORSE, *and* ONE THOUSAND DRAGOONS; *and* MAINTAIN THEM AT THEIR OWN CHARGE, *so long as it was necessary*. Besides this, they desired her majesty to *nominate officers* to command them.

AN address was, about the same time, presented to the queen, from above *ten thousand* of the *tinners of Cornwall*, "faithfully promising, NOTWITHSTANDING THE ARTI-
" FICES AND EVIL DESIGNS OF DISAFFECTED MEN, TO
" WITHDRAW THEM FROM THEIR LOYALTY, and unalter-
" able allegiance to Their Majesties, and the GLORIOUS
" CONSTITUTION *by* THEM *established* at the REVOLUTION,
" &c."

THE deputy lieutenants and officers of the militia, for Middlesex and Westminster, a few days after, made a solemn address and declaration, to the same purport as the lord mayor and aldermen.

IN such a juncture, the queen gave proofs of remarkable courage, activity, and discretion. She issued out proper orders and directions for putting the nation in a posture of defence, as well as for refitting and augmenting the fleet. She issued commissions to put the standing forces in condition to oppose the enemy; and she ordered the militia, in the western parts, to be in a readiness of defending the coasts, and assisting the army. Besides, TO STRIKE TERROR INTO THE CONSPIRATORS WITH FRANCE, she published a PROCLAMATON for apprehending several of the NOBILITY, GENTRY, and *others*, who had *conspired with many other* DISAFFECTED PERSONS, *to* DISTURB *and* DESTROY *the* GOVERNMENT; *and*, FOR THAT PURPOSE, *had* ABETTED *and* ADHERED *to* THEIR MAJESTIES' *enemies in the present* INVASION. But the French had suffered so much in the Netherlands, that they were forced, in spite of their victory over the English and Dutch fleets, to remain upon the defensive; and were not able to spare, at that moment, so many men as were necessary to effect a serious invasion of Great Britain.

THE only thing alarming, and which was much magnified, was, when they landed at Torbay. About a thousand of their men, without opposition, cannonaded and set fire to the village of Teigmouth, and burnt a few coasting vessels; after which they reimbarked, and returned to Brest.

THIS was the only alarming invasion since the conquest, that apparently could have been accomplished
without

without much difficulty. Had it taken place, there would have been an end of THAT CONSTITUTION, in its infancy, which we are now guarding with such zeal, against the GALLIC DISCIPLES of a MARAUDING and MURDERING PHILOSOPHY.

CHAP. X.

SECOND ATTEMPT OF LEWIS XIV. TO INVADE ENGLAND.

WHILE King William, in spring 1692, was employed on the Continent, in settling the warlike operations of the grand confederacy against France, Lewis XIV. resolved again to attempt the Invasion of England in his absence; and seemed heartily engaged in the interest of James, whose emissaries, in Britain, began to exert themselves with uncommon activity, in preparing their abettors, by a preparation of measures that would render such invasion successful.

THE Queen displayed, at this crisis, her usual vigilance, care, and spirit. She called out the Militia: She gave strict orders for the speedy equipping and sailing of the fleet: She sent over to Holland for three regiments of foot, which, with some troops remaining in the kingdom, formed a strong camp near Portsmouth: She published a Proclamation, to secure the kingdom from the dangers of insurrection, commanding all papists to depart from the metropolis, and not to remain within ten miles of it: She caused diligent search to be made after several disaffected persons, and committed some to the Tower, others to Newgate; and upon some concealing themselves, she issued a proclamation to discover and apprehend certain noblemen, gentlemen and others: She suddenly assembled parliament " for the
" safety

" safety of the kingdom, at a moment when the nation was
" threatened with a powerful invasion from abroad."

She ordered likewise the militia of Westminster, consisting of two regiments of foot, of ONE THOUSAND FIVE HUNDRED men each, and a troop of horse, to appear in Hyde Park, at a fixed day, under the command of the Lord Lieutenant, the Earl of Bedford. She ordered the trained bands of the City of London, also, containing six regiments, under the command of the Lord Mayor and their respective colonels, to repair to the same place, the day following. These alone amounted to about TEN THOUSAND MEN. Her Majesty, on both days, went in person to review them, and expressed herself extremely well satisfied with their appearance and DISCIPLINE; and the great zeal and promptitude which they displayed, for the service of their country. Indeed she adopted every measure, with the utmost vigour and wisdom, that might contribute to put the whole nation in a proper posture of defence.

Lewis, in the mean time, had acquainted the disaffected, with whom a close correspondence was kept up, that the projected invasion would take place on the coast of Sussex. So much precaution had been taken in France, to carry on the necessary preparations, that every thing was ready for executing the design, before it was so much as suspected in England. The land forces consisted of fourteen battalions of English and Irish, and NINE THOUSAND French, so that in all there could not be less than TWENTY THOUSAND men. THIRTY OR FORTY THOUSAND more, if necessary, was promised by the French king. A fleet of THREE HUNDRED transports was collected, and well provided with every thing necessary for the invasion. The troops were ready to embark, and only waited the arrival of Count d'Etrees, the admiral, with a squadron of twelve men of war, appointed

to

to escort the transports; while Admiral Tourville, the commander in chief, cruised in the Channel with the grand fleet, to cover the invasion.

The plan of James was, to march from Sussex, at the head of the above troops, and *push on directly for the* CAPITAL. They were to bring over only a small number of horses, *as the disaffected had undertaken to supply them with plenty on landing.* The French king, at the same time, was to march a large army into Flanders; and he seemed to imagine that the scheme was so well laid, that it was impossible to miscarry. Indeed he publicly said, before he set out, that he was going to put a speedy end to the war.

Although the queen had shewn great alacrity, as to putting the kingdom in a state of defence, her administration were very deficient in procuring intelligence. So little care had been taken in that essential matter, that if the winds had favoured the invaders, they themselves would have been the first to have brought over the circumstantial news of their design. A few days before they calculated that they should be on the English coast, they dispatched some of their agents to this country, in order to give private information to their treasonable abettors. But there luckily happened, for a whole month successively, such storms and contrary winds, that it was not possible for them to sail out of port; nor could d'Estrees come round from Toulon so soon as was expected with his squadron.

These storms and winds, fortunate for England, were perhaps the means, more than the action that happened afterwards, off La Hogue, that preserved the glorious Constitution of 1688, to the present, and we trust to future, generations. For in the interval of a month, the plot of the invasion became to be every day more unfolded, not only by
some

some of the supposed zealots, who disclosed it to government, but by many other certain proofs; so that in the beginning of May, about forty sail of the English fleet were on the coast of Normandy, endeavouring to destroy the French transports.

When the queen had received clear accounts of the plan of the invasion, besides her great preparations made at land, she ordered Admiral Russel to hasten out to sea immediately. Lewis, on the other hand, ordered the French admiral, Tourville, to attack the English, before they were joined by the Dutch fleet; and without even waiting for the Toulon squadron: And, in case of defeating Russel, James was ready to embark at La Hogue, with his invading army.

The English admiral sailed on the 11th of May, from Rye to St. Helen's, where he was joined by two more English squadrons; and soon afterwards, by the whole Dutch fleet. The combined fleets set sail on the 18th of May, consisting of 99 ships of the line, besides frigates and fire ships. About three o'clock the following morning, they discovered the French, under the Count de Tourville, and threw out the signal of battle. This was effected about eight o'clock, in good order; the Dutch in the van, the blue division in the rear, and the red in the center. The French did not exceed 63 ships of the line; and, as they were to windward, Tourville might have avoided an engagement; but he had received a positive order to fight, on the supposition, that the Dutch and English fleets had not joined. The French king, indeed, was apprised of their junction, before they were descried by his admiral, to whom he dispatched a countermanding order, by two several vessels; but, one of them was captured by the English, and the other did not arrive till the day after the engagement.

Tourville,

Tourville, therefore, in obedience to the firſt mandate, bore down along-ſide of Ruſſel's own ſhip, which he engaged at a very ſmall diſtance. He fought with great fury till one o'clock, when his rigging and ſails being conſiderably damaged, his ſhip, the Riſing Sun, that carried one hundred and four cannon, was towed out of the line, in great diſorder. Neverthelefs, the engagement continued till three, when the fleets were parted by a thick fog.

When this abated, the enemy were deſcried flying to the northward; and Ruſſel made the ſignal for chaſing. Part of the blue ſquadron came up with the enemy, about eight in the evening, and engaged them half an hour; during which, Admiral Carter was mortally wounded. Finding himſelf dying, he exhorted his captain to fight as long as the ſhip could ſwim; and expired with great compoſure. At length, the French bore away for Conquet Road, having loſt four ſhips in this day's action.

Next day, about eight in the morning, they were diſcovered, crowding away to the weſtward, and the combined fleets chaſed with all the ſail they could carry, until Ruſſel's fore-top-maſt came by the board. Though he was retarded by this accident, they ſtill continued the purſuit, and he anchored near cape La Hogue.

On the twenty-ſecond of the month, about ſeven in the morning, part of the French fleet was perceived near the Race of Alderney; ſome at anchor, and ſome driven to the eaſtward, with the tide of flood. He, and the ſhips neareſt him, immediately ſlipped their cables, and chaced. The Riſing Sun having loſt her maſts, ran aſhore near Cherbourg, where ſhe was burnt by Sir Ralph Delaval, together with the Admirable, another firſt-rate, and the Conquerant of eighty guns.

Eighteen

EIGHTEEN other ships of their fleet, ran into La Hogue where they were attacked by Sir George Rooke, who destroyed them, and a great number of transports, loaded with ammunition, in the midst of a terrible fire from the enemy, and in sight of the Irish camp.

SIR John Ashby, with his own squadron, and some Dutch ships, pursued the rest of the French fleet, which escaped through the Race of Alderney, by such a dangerous passage, as the English could not attempt, without exposing their ships to the most imminent danger.

THIS was a very mortifying defeat to the French king, who had been so long flattered with an uninterrupted series of victories, and reduced James to the lowest ebb of despondence, as it frustrated the whole scheme of his embarkation, and overwhelmed his friends, in England, with grief and despair.

RUSSEL acted in the whole of this expedition, with the genuine spirit of a British Admiral. He plyed from the Nore to the Downs with a very scanty wind through the dangerous sands, contrary to the advice of all his pilots; and, by this bold passage, effected a junction of the different squadrons, which otherwise the French would have attacked singly, and perhaps defeated. He behaved with great gallantry during the engagement; he destroyed about fifteen of the enemy's capital ships. In a word, he obtained such a decisive victory, that during the remaining part of the war, the French would not hazard another battle by sea, with the English.

THE queen was so well pleased with the victory, that she ordered 30,000l. to be distributed among the sailors; medals to be struck in honour of the battle; and the bodies of Admiral Carter and Captain Haſtings, who had been killed in the fight, to be interred with great funeral pomp.

PREVIOUS to each of the engagements off *Beachy Head*, in 1690, and at *La Hogue*, in 1692, it appears that the Engliſh were equally remiſs for want of intelligence. In other reſpects, the advantages and diſadvantages of both were ſomewhat ſimilar. Torrington fought the French with a much inferior force againſt the opinion of himſelf and officers, by command of the queen, and was vanquiſhed. Tourville engaged Ruſſel, with nearly the ſame diſadvantages, two years thereafter, as Torrington had before fought him; and againſt the opinion of his officers, owing to the commands, too, of his Sovereign, and was likewiſe beaten. The Plymouth diviſion could not join Torrington, nor the Toulon diviſion join Tourville in time, owing to contrary winds. But then it muſt be confeſſed, that in the firſt engagement, as in the laſt, Tourville brought his whole force into action; whereas, in Ruſſel's engagement with that Admiral, the combined fleets of England and Holland were not half of them in the engagement. Another incident is remarkable; and it has been very often the ſlanderous and malevolent drawback upon many great victories, particularly at ſea; namely, *that moſt commanders could have done more than they accompliſhed*. Tourville, after his defeat of Torrington, was blamed by the Jacobites, for not making the moſt of his victory. So it happened, to Admiral Ruſſel: So it happened, on the deciſive 12th of April to the gallant Rodney. *So it happened lately, in the affair of Toulon, to the brave and ſkilful Lord Hood*. Therefore every great man muſt occaſionally expect that the tongue of envious calumny will mix this baſe alloy with his merit; and undervalue his ſuperior genius, and his diſtinguiſhed ability, when crowned by good fortune.

THIS great and decisive action off La Hogue, gave such a mortal blow to the NAVY of France, in the LAST century, as *the late* DESTRUCTION *of their* SHIPPING *in the harbour of* TOULON *has done in the* PRESENT; *the effects of which, in spite of all their* MISREPRESENTATIONS *and their* BOASTINGS, *will be severely felt by the French for* A CENTURY HEREAFTER; WHATEVER GOVERNMENT *may take place in that* DISTRACTED *and* RESTLESS *country,* hitherto ALWAYS INIMICAL *to the* LIBERTIES *and the* REPOSE *of Europe.*

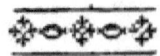

CHAP. XI.

THIRD ATTEMPT AT INVASION, BY LEWIS XIV.

WHEN the French monarch endeavoured, by a third attempt, to invade England, early in the spring, in 1708, and place the doubtful son of James upon the throne of these kingdoms, his navy was much diminished, and had lost all its former terrors. The battle of La Hogue had destroyed its great and dangerous power. Ever since that fortunate event, and the affair at Vigo, in 1702, where eight sail of the line, two of 62, two of 60, two of 56, and two of 46 guns, besides frigates and galleons, were burnt or taken, belonging to France; instead of seeing its navy riding on our coasts, we sent every year a powerful fleet to insult theirs; superior to them, not only in the ocean, but in the Mediterranean. We had established our reputation, in the reign of Queen Anne, so effectually, as the first maritime power, that we feel, even at this day, the happy effects of that fame which we then acquired.

Lewis was so exasperated at our attack upon Toulon, the year preceding, which we would have certainly carried, had it not been for the tardiness of the Duke of Savoy, that he meant to retaliate, by another invasion in favour of the Pretender. Had the blow at Toulon been struck,

struck, the maritime power of France would have been totally extinguished; as there were then in that harbour, a fleet of 26 sail of the line, 11 ships of 62 and 60 guns, and nine of between 58 and 50 guns, besides many smaller vessels. But although the English did not capture that important place, they destroyed one ship of 90 guns, one of 86, one of 82, one of 70, two of 60, and one of 54 guns; besides damaging a great number of others, blowing up several magazines, destroying 160 houses, and the allies committing great devastations in Provence.

The union, too, had been recently made between the two kingdoms, and the French king expected that a powerful faction would be raised in Scotland, in favour of his puppet the Pretender, owing to the inconsiderate dissatisfaction of the Scotch at that event.

The true scheme of Lewis, by this invasion, or rather descent, as his fleet, on the expedition, consisted but of eight men of war, was to create a commotion in England, and a rebellion in Scotland; that, by means of trials and executions, Queen Anne and her ministry might be sufficiently embarrassed at home, and have the less leisure to prosecute their warlike views abroad. And, from these motives, he ordered his ministers, in all foreign courts, to talk in very magnificent terms, of the succours he gave to the King of England, as he thought fit to call the Pretender; that, on the rebound, they might make the louder noise in Britain, and induce us to believe our danger the greater, and more inevitable.

The politics of the French monarch, in this respect, had their effect; for, on General Cadogan's sending over an express, disclosing the whole design, the queen, by Mr. Secretary Boyle, acquainted the House of Commons with this new project of invasion, and received a very

loyal

loyal address from them, as well as from the Lords; but the apprehensions expressed in England, had such an effect upon the monied interest, that it occasioned a prodigious run upon the Bank, and very much disturbed our foreign remittances.

This run upon the Bank, so much alarmed the Exchequer, that all ways and means possible were concerted, to put an immediate stop to it; in order to which, the Lord High Treasurer not only allowed six, instead of three per cent. for all the money circulating by their bills, but also supplied them with large sums of money, out of his own private fortune. This example being followed by the Dukes of Marlborough, Newcastle, Somerset, and other noblemen, with the calling in of 20 per cent. upon their capital, the panic was dispelled, and credit regained its wonted confidence much sooner than it could have been expected.

The HOUSE OF COMMONS came to a very *proper* and *salutary* RESOLUTION, " *That whoever* DESIGNEDLY *endea-*
" *voured to* DESTROY *or* LESSEN *the* PUBLIC CREDIT, *especially*
" *at a time when the kingdom was* THREATENED *with* AN
" INVASION, *was* GUILTY *of a* HIGH CRIME *and* MISDE-
" MEANOUR, *and was an* ENEMY *to* HER MAJESTY *and* HER
" KINGDOMS.

Let the MONIED INTEREST, in like cases, never be alarmed, and ruin themselves by their timidity. In the crisis of the most formidable and desperate invasion that imbecility and tremor can imagine, the stock-holders, for their own safety, ought to remain FIRM and TRANQUIL. If they endeavour, then, *by great runs on their bankers, and every other method that fear can suggest,* to REALIZE THEIR SECURITIES, they will *inevitably bring ruin on themselves.* In such a moment, it should be their chief business

to

to place all their CONFIDENCE in GOVERNMENT, and lend every possible aid to strengthen its arm. As well might we expect, by flight in the face of the enemy, on the eve of battle, to secure ourselves and kindred from his devastation, as by drawing out our monied property, even in an actual invasion, to obtain it for our lasting benefit.

THE truth is, although there be money enough, in the day of confidence, to answer every possible demand; yet, could that confidence be once withdrawn, which the good sense of the nation never can permit, as there is not, nor ever was, nor ever will be, money sufficient to pay off all the public creditors AT ONCE, a national bankruptcy would take place; the monied people would be ruined; and, if the foe had then made good a landing, the whole kingdom would be thrown into an irrecoverable convulsion.

BUT, as the resources of this country are immense; by our having *a firm reliance on* GOVERNMENT, *in the day of danger, and giving every support to public credit, at such a moment, we would* DISCOMFIT *the enemy, however mighty, protect our* PROPERTY, *preserve our* LIBERTY, *and save our envied and unparalleled* CONSTITUTION, *from the merciless dagger of* GALLIC ASSASSINATION.

OUR public securities, and all kinds of property, fell surprizingly in value, by the arts of the French, and *the traitors at home*, on this rumoured invasion in 1708; and the kingdom was on the brink of general confusion, if the panic had not happily very quickly subsided.

BESIDES the exertions of the above spirited noblemen, and the Resolution of the House of Commons, the nation was much indebted, for its speedy and tranquil recovery,

to

to the alacrity of the Admiralty, who fitted out a fleet of twenty-four men of war, with remarkable diligence.

Lewis began to make preparations for this expedition at Dunkirk, where a squadron of eight ships was assembled, under the command of the Chevalier de Fourbin; and a body of about twelve battalions, of land forces, were embarked with Monsieur de Gace.

The Pretender was furnished with services of gold and silver plate, sumptuous tents, rich clothes for his life guards, splendid liveries, and all sorts of necessaries, even to profusion. The French king, at parting, presented him with a sword, studded with valuable diamonds, and repeated what he had formerly said to James, in like cases, " I hope I shall never see you again." The Pope contributed to the expence of this expedition, and accommodated him with various religious mottos, which were wrought upon his colours and standards.

The Queen and the Parliament, mean while, adopted the most vigourous measures. Among other steps, they suspended the *Habeas Corpus* act for some months, with respect to persons apprehended by the government, on suspicion of treasonable practices; while ten battalions of the British forces were ordered from the Netherlands. The Pretender and his adherents, were proclaimed traitors and rebels; and the English fleet, under Sir George Byng, sailed from Deal, towards Dunkirk. The French, imagining that our fleets were abroad, and Britain unprovided with ships of war, were amazed and confounded when such a powerful squadron appeared off Mardyke. A stop was immediately put to the embarkation of their troops. Frequent expresses were dispatched to Paris. The French Admiral represented to his master, the little probability of succeeding in this enterprize,

prize, and the danger that would attend the attempt. But he received positive orders to proceed.

The British fleet being forced, on the fourteenth of March, from their station, by severe weather, the French squadron sailed on the seventeenth, from the Road of Dunkirk; but the wind shifting, it anchored in Newport Pits, till the nineteenth, in the evening, when they set sail again, with a fair breeze, steering their course for Scotland. Sir George Byng, having received advice of their departure, from an Ostend vessel, sent out for that purpose, by Major General Cadogan, gave chace to the enemy; after having detached a squadron, under Admiral Baker, to convoy the troops that were embarked at Ostend for England.

The queen, in consequence of this, went to the house of Peers, where, in a speech to both houses, she told them the French fleet had sailed; that Sir George Byng was in pursuit of them; and that ten battalions of her troops were expected every day in England. This intimation was followed by two very warm addresses from the Lords and Commons, in which they repeated their assurances, of defending her against all her enemies; exhorted her to persevere in supporting the common cause, notwithstanding this petty attempt to disturb her dominions; and levelled some severe insinuations against those who endeavoured to foment jealousies, between her majesty and her most faithful servants.

Addresses, on the same occasion, were sent up from different parts of the kingdom; so that the queen seemed to look with contempt on the designs of the enemy. Several regiments of foot, with some squadrons of cavalry, began their march from Scotland; while the Earl of Leven, commander in chief of the forces in that country, and governor of the Castle of Edinburgh, hastened thither to put that fortress in a posture of defence, and to make the proper dispositions to oppose the Pretender, at his landing.

But the vigilance of Sir George Byng, rendered all these precautions unnecessary. He sailed directly to the Frith of Edinburgh, where he arrived almost as soon as the enemy, who immediately took the advantage of a land-breeze, and bore away with all the sail they could carry. The English admiral gave chace; and the Salisbury, one of their ships, was boarded and taken. At night, Monsieur de Fourbin altered his course; so that, next day, they were out of reach of the English squadron.

The Pretender desired they would proceed to the northward, and land him at Inverness; and Fourbin seemed willing to grant this request; but, the wind changing, and blowing in their teeth with great violence, he represented the danger of attempting to prosecute the voyage; and, with his consent, and that of his general, after having been tossed about a whole month, in very tempestuous weather, they returned to Dunkirk.

The intended invasion was thus totally defeated, without having the least bad effects on our affairs, if we except a temporary shock upon the public mind; but which only united us the more, in favour of the *admirable system of* GOVERNMENT, ESTABLISHED *at* THE REVOLUTION; and CONFIRMED the *antipathy* of THE NATION *against* FRANCE, as to any FUTURE INTERFERENCE regarding the CONSTITUTION of GREAT BRITAIN.

CHAP.

CHAP. XII.

OF THE THREATENED INVASION FROM FRANCE, IN 1715; FROM SWEDEN, IN 1717; FROM SPAIN, IN 1718; AND OF A CONSPIRACY TO PROMOTE AN INSURRECTION, AND INVASION, IN 1722.

OF THE ATTEMPT IN 1715.

THE illustrious HOUSE of HANOVER, had scarcely ascended the throne, as *guardians* of the LIBERTIES OF BRITAIN, than a rebellion, in favour of the Pretender, broke out in Scotland, in 1715, but was speedily crushed, without much bloodshed. The Pretender did not arrive there till after the decisive battle of Sheriff-Muir, in a small and solitary vessel, from Dunkirk, that had formerly been a privateer of eight guns, without any foreign aid whatever accompanying him; and was soon after obliged to return to France. It is unnecessary to record this expedition circumstantially, as it cannot properly be deemed an invasion, according to the plan of our history; although it for a moment considerably alarmed the country.

GEORGE I. who was endowed by nature with an extensive genius, cultivated by an excellent education, and great experience; long known and esteemed by the English nation, for his valour and good conduct; adopted every measure to render the rebellion abortive.

THE parliament and the great body of the people displayed their loyalty and zeal, too, upon this occasion, in an effectual manner. An act was passed, impowering the king to *secure all* SUSPECTED PERSONS, and to *suspend the* HABEAS CORPUS *act in that moment of peril*. A reward of 100,000l. was offered for the Pretender, dead or alive. Sir George Byng was ordered to take the command of the fleet. Portsmouth was put into a state of defence. The guards were encamped in Hyde Park. Thirteen regiments of dragoons, and eight of infantry, were ordered to be raised. The trained bands were kept in readiness to suppress tumults; and the vigilance of government, aided by the great exertions of the Duke of Argyle, soon defeated this faint attempt, to destroy the CONSTITUTION, as established at the REVOLUTION.

OF THE ATTEMPT OF SWEDEN, IN 1717.

No sooner was this rebellion extinguished, than the plan of an invasion, of a serious nature, was providentially detected. Charles XII. of Sweden, enraged at the English monarch, for purchasing the Duchies of Bremen and Verden, and which he would by no means relinquish, breathed nothing but revenge. He formed a design, in conjunction with the Pretender, of invading Britain; and

to

to set aside the House of Hanover, by placing him on that throne. The ministers of Sweden, resident at London, Paris, and the Hague, maintained a correspondence with the disaffected subjects of Great Britain. With a view to avert this danger, or to prepare against it, the king went to the Continent; and in a few days after his return to London, he ordered the Swedish minister, Count Gyllenberg, to be seized, and his papers secured. This was effectually performed, by General Wade and Colonel Blakeney. Two gentlemen were also apprehended, on suspicion of being in confederacy with the ambassador.

Baron Gortz, the Swedish resident in Holland, was, about the same time, seized with his papers, by order of the States, through the influence of the king. The Baron owned, that he had projected the invasion; and that he had provided arms for 10,000 men, and other necessaries. By their papers, which were laid before parliament, it appeared, that a design was formed to dethrone his majesty; and which was conducted in such an artful manner, that had it not been owing to his own vigilance, wisdom, and spirit, there was great probability of its having been attended with success.

Like Chauvelin, Count Gyllenberg descended to the meanest arts. Pamphlets, *through his means, were published, to* foment *and* increase discontent *and* division. *He himself wrote seditious essays, in the papers of that day. The tranquility enjoyed in Britain, was to be the occasion of* requiring *and* obtaining *the* reduction *of the* national, *and the* dismission *of the* foreign forces. *Every trick that has been played by* certain persons, *in a* high sphere, *for these last two years, to excite* sedition *and* tumult, *was then practised, and not without success.*

While

WHILE these schemes were operating in Britain, ships, purchased at different places, were to assemble, in March, at Gottenburgh, when the east winds usually blow; on board of which, 8000 foot, and 4000 horse were to embark, with artillery, arms, and ammunition, for 15,000 men.

THE King of Sweden having sent full power to his ambassadors, which were shewn to the leaders of the sedition, this removed all uneasiness and irresolution. Money was given. Views were explained. Means of subsisting the foreign troops were settled. A person, who was perfectly well acquainted with the coasts, where it was fixed that the troops should land, was engaged. Ships of war were provided, from 60 to 70 guns. Merchant vessels, that were to carry corn to Gottenburgh, were to serve as transports. The plan was artfully laid, and the execution deemed infallible, *if the country could be persuaded by the traiterous attempts at home to* REDUCE *the* ARMY, *and send the* FOREIGN AUXILIARIES *that were then here, belonging to Holland, out of the kingdom.*

TWELVE THOUSAND *chosen Swedes,* landing with such a quantity of spare arms for the use of the seditious that would be ready to join them; aided by the powerful engine of an abandoned press, corrupting, misleading, and destroying the virtuous energy of the public mind; a powerful army would have been quickly formed in England. The Scotch, those violent and heedless dupes of selfish leaders, in most ages, would have all been in arms. The torrent would have rapidly increased without ceasing; a battle would have taken place, and the admirable fabrick of 1688, probably been laid low in one vast ruin.

BUT the PENETRATION and the MEASURES of THE KING, *saved the country;* and the formidable Swedish monarch was soon

soon after slain. Every friend to the Constitution extolled the king's wisdom and his conduct. It was a pleasing reflection to the English nation, when they beheld *the* CHIEF *of a* FAMILY *destined to secure their* RELIGIOUS *and* CIVIL LIBERTIES, *giving such* EARLY PROOFS *of his* CAPACITY *since the commencement of his reign;* to PRESERVE *their* RIGHTS *with such spirit, and his* THRONE *with such policy and firmness.*

OF THE ATTEMPT OF SPAIN, IN 1718.

On the death of Lewis XIV. his successor, Lewis XV. being a minor, the regency devolved on the Duke of Orleans. This event made a wonderful alteration in the cabinets of St James's and Versailles. The English monarch knew that the Duke resolved to ascend the throne of France, in case the young King, who was a sickly child, should die without issue. As Philip King of Spain, the grandson of Lewis XIV. had renounced all claim to the French crown, the Duke of Orleans was the presumptive heir. But the king was not ignorant that Philip would powerfully contest that succession, notwithstanding his renunciation; and that the Regent would be glad of any opportunity to strengthen his interest by an alliance with the maritime powers of England and Holland. The King, through General Cadogan, sounded the Duke on this subject, and found him eager to engage in such an alliance. A treaty between England, France and Holland was soon accomplished. The Pretender and all his adherents by that treaty, were to be driven out of France. Dunkirk was to be demolished. A mutual guarantee of all the places possessed by the contracting powers, of the Protestant succession on the throne of England, and of

the

the Duke of Orleans, in cafe of the death of the King without iſſue, to the throne of France. A reciprocal aid of ſhips and troops was to be furniſhed to that power which ſhould be invaded from abroad, or diſturbed at home. And the Regent bound himſelf to do *" whatever the King of Great Britain might judge neceſſary to remove his fuſ- picions."*

THE Spaniſh Monarch was much hurt at this alliance; and from that moment he embraced every meaſure that could diſconcert it. Being at war with the Emperor, he invaded and ſubdued Sardinia; and the next year, he reduced the greateſt part of the iſland of Sicily. On this a quadruple alliance was formed againſt Spain, by the Emperor, and the three before-mentioned powers.

THE King of England, jealous of the great and increaſing naval power of Spain, that threatened the liberties of Italy, and the peace of Europe, ſent out a powerful ſquadron, to the Mediterranean, under the command of Sir George Byng. It conſiſted of 20 ſail of the line, and one of 50 guns. The Spaniards, whoſe fleet amounted to 27 ſail, beſides gallies, fire-ſhips, bomb-veſſels, and ſtoreſhips; no ſooner perceived Sir George near Meſſina, than they bore away, but formed themſelves in order of battle. Next morning the engagement began, when they were all burnt or taken, except three ſhips of the line, and three frigates.

WE cannot reſiſt the impulſe of recording an anecdote of Captain Walton, who commanded the Canterbury in this expedition. Having been ordered, on the morning of the engagement, to give chace with ſix ſhips, to eight ſhips of the enemy, who were ſheering off with all the gallies, fire-ſhips, bomb-veſſels, and ſtore-ſhips; in a few days

days thereafter, Sir George received from him, the following LACONIC epistle:

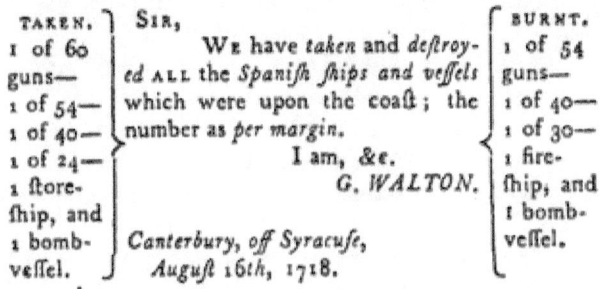

TAKEN.		BURNT.
1 of 60 guns—	SIR,	1 of 54 guns—
1 of 54—	We have *taken* and *destroyed* ALL the *Spanish ships and vessels* which were upon the coast; the number as *per margin*.	1 of 40—
1 of 40—		1 of 30—
1 of 24—		1 fireship, and
1 storeship, and	I am, &c.	1 bombvessel.
1 bombvessel.	G. WALTON.	
	Canterbury, off Syracuse,	
	August 16th, 1718.	

This will be a perpetual MODEL to all victorious officers, for its *brevity*, for its *perspicuity*, and for its *modesty*.

THE King of Spain was so enraged at the loss of his fleet, that he immediately meditated revenge. Cardinal Alberoni, his minister, formed a plan to seize and put an end to the power of the Regent, which was frustrated by the English monarch, from his superior intelligence, in giving him notice of his danger. The Regent, in return for that favour, acquainted the king with some hints of a scheme of the Spanish minister, *to invade* GREAT BRITAIN.

CONFERENCES had been frequently held, between the Cardinal and the exiled Duke of Ormond; who, at this time, resided in Spain. It was agreed to give the Pretender an invitation to Madrid, and put him at the head of a large body of auxiliary forces, which his catholic majesty proposed to lend him, in order to assert, with success, his pretensions to the throne of Britain. He accordingly quitted the dominions of the Pope, where he had taken refuge since his expulsion from France, and was received by the chagrined

grined Philip, with great marks of friendship; who, for his own purposes, entertained him with all the rank and the marks of respect due to the King of England.

The squadron that had been for some time fitting out for this expedition, *sailed for England, upon the Pretender's arrival at Madrid. It consisted of ten men of war, and transports, on board of which were* SIX THOUSAND *regular troops, chiefly Irish, with arms for* TEN *or* TWELVE THOUSAND MEN.

Some forces were ordered to the north, and the west of England, when the rumour of the invasion increased. Rewards were offered for seizing the Duke of Ormond, and the rest of his followers. The naval armament, against Spain, was prepared with great assiduity. And, upon the repeated advices of the Regent of France, the king came to the House of Peers, and acquainted the parliament with the intentions of the Spanish monarch.

Both houses *assured him of* THEIR SUPPORT. *The* COMMONS *desired him to* AUGMENT HIS FORCES BY SEA AND LAND, IN SUCH A MANNER AS HE SHOULD THINK FIT, *and promising to make good any increase of expence which might occur on that account.*

With these assurances, the King had the satisfaction to see his allies exert their zeal in his defence. The States General sent over 2000 men. The Governor of the Austrian Netherlands sent six battalions of Imperialists. The Regent of France offered twenty battalions, but it was not thought proper to accept them.

These, and many more precautions of the King, and the Nation, were wise and proper; but, as it happened, they proved needless. When the Spanish fleet arrived as far as Cape Finisterre, with a fair wind, a violent storm

arose

arose, that lasted two days and two nights. The fleet was entirely dispersed, and totally disabled from pursuing their course; and the Admiral's ship having lost all her masts, made for the coast of Spain, as did the rest of the fleet, except two frigates that arrived in Scotland with a few hundred Spanish troops, who afterwards surrendered themselves as prisoners of war. Thus terminated Cardinal Alberoni's, invasion of Great Britain.

OF THE CONSPIRACY, IN 1722, TO PROMOTE INSURRECTION AND INVASION.

THE means taken by the executive power, to defeat the conspiracy in 1722, having been lately adopted, in a great degree, by government; and Mr. Fox having denied that any *precedents* could be adduced for a COMMITTEE OF SECRECY, in like cases, the Chancellor of the Exchequer referred him to that conspiracy; and added, that he could cite a variety of other precedents to prove that such committees had often been formed by parliament, previous to that period.

A SECRET COMMITTEE was held, in 1679, to investigate the Popish plot. Another in 1715, for examining the papers relating to the peace of Utrecht. A third, in 1721, for enquiring into the South Sea affair. And a fourth, in 1722, for investigating the following conspiracy:

IN the beginning of May, that year, the king received information from his steady friend, the Regent of France, that another plot was formed against his crown, and the liberties

liberties of his people. The plan of the conspirators, was, to *seize the* COMMANDER IN CHIEF *and* THE TOWER. *Afterwards to possess themselves of the* BANK OF ENGLAND, *the* EXCHEQUER, *and all other places where the* PUBLIC MONEY *was lodged. And then to seize on the sacred person of* HIS MAJESTY, *and that of* THE PRINCE OF WALES; *bring over the Pretender, and* OVERTURN THE CONSTITUTION.

THEIR mode to effect this, was by procuring *a regular body of* FOREIGN TROOPS *to* INVADE BRITAIN, during the constitutional hilarity and division of sentiment accompanying the GENERAL ELECTION, which happened in March. But being disappointed in this expectation, it was resolved, that when the King went to Hanover that summer, which he intended, they were to attempt it, *by the help of such officers and soldiers as could pass into England, unobserved, from abroad, under the command of the Duke of Ormond; who was to have landed in the river with a great quantity of arms, provided in Spain; and, the Tower being seized, it was to become their arsenal.*

DISAPPOINTED also in this design, by the King receiving intelligence of the conspiracy; delaying his journey; forming immediately a camp in Hyde Park; ordering all military officers to join their regiments; sending for troops from Ireland; desiring the guarantee troops from the States General; sending to the Regent to be prepared with a force in case of necessity; seizing a number of suspected persons in Scotland; acquainting the Lord Mayor of London of the plot; that city and many other cities and towns pouring in loyal addresses; the conspirators, notwithstanding all these formidable preparations, would not relinquish, but defer their enterprize till the breaking up of the camps.

DURING that interval, they were labouring by their agents and emissaries, with all the *effrontery* and *cunning*
of

of MODERN JACOBINS, *to poison the minds of the people; to corrupt and seduce the* OFFICERS *and* SOLDIERS *of the army:* and they depended so much on the exciting a general defection and revolt by the following winter, as to entertain sanguine hopes of effecting their horrid purpose, although they should receive no assistance from abroad, but which they still fondly expected.

WHAT emboldened the disaffected in England was, that although the outline of the plot was known in May, none of them were taken into custody, until the latter end of summer, when many were seized.

BUT the reason of this was, government having adopted every step for the security of the country against all sudden attempts, they were induced from motives of policy to defer seizing any persons until the long vacation, as the conspirators would otherwise have received the benefit of the *Habeas Corpus* act; and thus, by their liberation before the whole plot was sifted to the bottom, the salutary intentions of government would have been in a considerable degree defeated.

THE new parliament was assembled in October, when the King made a long and excellent speech, acquainting both houses of the conspiracy. Among other admirable remarks in it, so descriptive of the PATRIOTIC ACTIONS of our PRESENT WORTHY SOVEREIGN; his GREAT ANCESTOR then said:

" *Had I, since my* ACCESSION *to the* THRONE, *ever at-*
" *tempted any* INNOVATION IN OUR ESTABLISHED RELIGION
" —*Had I*, IN ANY ONE INSTANCE, INVADED *the* LIBERTY
" *and* PROPERTY *of my subjects—I should less wonder at*
" *any endeavours to alienate the affections of my people, and*
" DRAW

" DRAW THEM INTO MEASURES THAT CAN END IN NOTHING
" BUT THEIR OWN DESTRUCTION."

We cannot help quoting part of the addrefs of the commons, to the King, on that occafion; as it depicts CERTAIN PERSONS, and their NEFARIOUS DESIGNS, in fuch a glaring point of view, that in beholding the political picture of that day, we cannot but perceive a very ftrong refemblance to a hideous one of the prefent period. It was this:

" WE cannot exprefs too great an abhorrence of fuch
" unnatural practices, nor too great an indignation againft
" thofe *who would have made the capital of this flourifhing*
" *kingdom, a fcene of blood and defolation.*

" WICKED MEN! *whilft they have the malice to revile* YOUR
" GOVERNMENT, *and attempt to* OVERTURN IT; *at the fame*
" *time, they have the* INSOLENCE *to depend upon the* CLEMENCY
" *of it for their* SECURITY.

" WHILE THEY are *endeavouring to* DESTROY ALL LIBER-
" TY, *they are clamouring that a few of them are, for the*
" PUBLIC SAFETY, CONFINED.

" WHILE THEY are *attempting to* DESTROY ALL PRO-
" PERTY, *they are* MURMURING *at the* NECESSARY TAXES
" *given to your* MAJESTY *for the* SECURITY *of it. And,*
" *whilft they* ACT againft ALL LAW THEMSELVES, *they* TRUST
" *and are* CONFIDENT *that, even in their own cafes, the*
" LAWS *of the Realm will be the rule and meafure of your*
" *actions.*"

The parliament immediately proceeded to *fufpend* the *Habeas Corpus* act, for ONE YEAR. This was violently oppofed by the *diffaffected*, on a pretence that it endangered

dangered public liberty, becaufe it defeated their machinations. A SECRET COMMITTEE, of the Houfe of Commons was chofen, with full power, to examine into the confpiracy; and, after confining fome noblemen and gentlemen; banifhing the Bifhop of Rochefter, and executing Layer, a lawyer; the Duke of Norfolk, Lord North and Grey, Lord Orrery, and the others imprifoned upon that affair, were, through the clemency of his Majefty, pardoned and liberated; and the whole fcheme of that attrocious plot was defeated.

CHAP. XIII.

OF THE PROJECTED INVASION, IN 1743, BY FRANCE.

BRITAIN had been free from all menaces of invasion or alarming insurrection for twenty-one years, when, *by the violence of parliamentry disputes, by the loud clamours of many,* AND HEIGHTENED BY THE TREACHEROUS INTRIGUES OF THE DISAFFECTED, the ministry of France were persuaded that the nation was ripe for a revolt.

THIS belief was cherished and corroborated by the assertions of their indefatigable emissaries, in different parts of the three kingdoms. *These were men of strong prejudices, and warm imaginations, who saw things through the medium of discontent, sordid motives, violent passions, and the heat of party. They spoke rather from extravagant zeal to overturn the constitution, and introduce popery, slavery, and arbitrary power,* THAT THEY AND THEIR FRIENDS MIGHT RULE; *than from any sober conviction that their plan could be accomplished.*

THEY gave the court of Versailles to understand, that if the Pretender, whom they stiled the Chevalier de St. George, or his eldest son, Charles Edward, then about 23 years of age, should appear at the head of a French army in Great Britain, a revolution would instantly follow in his favour.

THIS

This intimation was agreeable to Cardinal de Tencin, who had succeeded the amiable, the politic, and the pacific Cardinal Fleury, as Prime Minister of France. As for that warm friend of the House of Hanover, the Duke of Orleans, the Regent, he had been dead twenty years. Tencin was of a violent temper. He had been recommended to the people by the Pretender, and was warmly attached to his interest. His ambition was flattered with a prospect of performing services to his benefactor, and by that means to the Catholic faith. He foresaw that if even his aim should miscarry, an invasion of Great Britain would make a considerable diversion from the continent, by the withdrawing of our troops, and assist France, with which we were than engaged in hostilities. It would besides embroil and embarras his Britannic Majesty, George II. who was the chief support of the House of Austria, and its allies. Tencin, actuated by these motives, concerted measures with the Pretender at Rome, who being too much advanced in years to engage in such an expedition, agreed to delegate his pretensions and his mock authority to his son Charles.

Count Saxe, one of the greatest generals of the age, was appointed by the French King to command the troops designed for this expedition, which amounted to 15,000 men. They began their march to Picardy, and a great number of vessels were assembled for their embarkation, at DUNKIRK, CALAIS, and BOULOGNE. *It was determined that they should be* LANDED *in* KENT, *under convoy of a* STRONG SQUADRON, EQUIPPED AT BREST, and commanded by Monsieur de Roquefeuille, an officer of experience and capacity.

Matters being thus prepared, Charles departed from Rome about the end of December, incognito, in the disguise of a Spanish courier, attended by one servant only,

only, and furnished with the proper passports. He travelled through Tuscany to Genoa, from whence he proceeded to Savona, where he embarked for Antibes; and, prosecuting his journey to Paris, was indulged with a private audience of the French King. He then set out, still concealing his identity, for the coast of Picardy.

M. de Roquefeuille, in the month of January, sailed from Brest, directing his course up the English Channel, with a fleet of twenty sail. They were immediately discovered by a cruiser, which ran into Plymouth, and the intelligence was instantly conveyed by express to the board of Admiralty. Sir John Norris was ordered to take the command of the fleet at Spithead, with which he sailed to the Downes, where he was joined by some ships of the line from Chatham; and then he found himself at the head of a squadron considerably stronger than that of the enemy.

MEANWHILE, the kingdom was put in a posture of defence. Several regiments marched to the west of England. All governors and commanders were ordered to repair immediately to their respective posts. The forts at the north of the Thames, and the Medway were strengthened and prepared against every attack. Directions were issued to assemble the Kentish Militia, to defend the coast in case of an invasion. His Majesty, by message to both Houses of Parliament, acquainted them of the arrival of the Pretender's son in France; the preparations at Dunkirk, and the appearance of the French fleet in the English Channel.

THEY joined in an address, assuring him, that they would, with the warmest zeal and unanimity, take such measures as would enable him to frustrate and defeat so desperate and insolent an attempt. Addresses of the same nature

were

were prefented by the city of London, both univerfities, the principal towns in Great Britain, the clergy, the diffenting minifters, the quakers, and almoft all the corporations and communities of the kingdom. The States General granted their auxiliary aid of 6000 troops, with great alacrity and expedition. The Earl of Stair, and OTHER OPPOSITIONISTS of that day, offered their fervices to government; which, as they were tendered with *an honeft patriot zeal*, were received with a becoming confidence and affection. Orders were fent to Flanders to bring over fix thoufand of the Britifh troops, in cafe the invafion fhould actually take place. The Parliament, in another addrefs, exhorted the King to augment his forces by fea and land. The *Habeas Corpus* act was *fufpended* for SIX MONTHS. *Several perfons of diftinction were apprehended, on fufpicion of* TREASONABLE PRACTICES. All papifts and nonjurors were commanded, by proclamation, to retire ten miles from London; and every precaution was taken that feemed neceffary for the prefervation of the public tranquility.

THE French court, meanwhile, proceeded with their preparations at Boulogne and Dunkirk, under the eye of the young Pretender; and 7000 men were actually embarked. M. de Roquefeuille failed up the Channel, as far as Dungenefs, a promontory on the coaft of Kent; after having detached five fhips under M. de Bareil, to haften the embarkation at Dunkirk.

WHILE the French Admiral anchored off Dungenefs, he perceived, on the 24th of February, the Britifh fleet doubling the South Foreland, from the Downes; and, though the wind was againft it, taking the opportunity of the tide, to come up and engage the French fquadron. Roquefeuille, who little expected fuch a vifit, could not be altogether compofed, confidering the great fuperiority of his enemy; but

but the tide failing, the English admiral was obliged to anchor two leagues short of the foe.

In this interval, M. de Roquefeuille called a council of war, in which it was determined to avoid an engagement, weigh anchor at sun-set, and make the best of their way to the place from whence they had set sail. This resolution was favoured by a very hard gale of wind, which began to blow from the north east, and carried them down the Channel with great expedition.

This storm, however, which in all probability, saved their fleet from destruction, utterly disconcerted the design of invading England. A great number of their transports were driven ashore, and destroyed; and the rest so damaged, that they could not be speedily repaired. The English were now masters at sea, and the coast was so well guarded, that the invasion could not be prosecuted, with any probability of success.

The French generals, nominated to serve in the expedition, returned to Paris; and the Pretender resolved to wait another opportunity, which happened in the following year: but terminated with so much bloodshed and disaster, that it ought to have destroyed the hopes of him and his adherents for ever, as to any conquest of these kingdoms, by future insurrections, and future invasions.

CHAP. XIV.

OF THE REBELLION IN 1745. AND THE MENACED INVASION OF FRANCE, IN 1755, 1756, 1758, AND 1759.

OF THE REBELLION, IN 1745.

AS the Rebellion raised by the young Pretender, was not accompanied by any naval invasion, we shall pass it slightly over. It is only necessary to remark here, that when news was received in London of his landing in Scotland, the King arrived in a few weeks thereafter from abroad, and every measure was adopted to defeat the machinations of the rebels.

A requisition was made for the Dutch auxiliaries. Several British regiments were recalled from the continent. Orders were issued to keep the trained bands in readiness; to array the militia of Westminster; and instructions to the same effect were sent to all the Lords Lieutenants of the counties throughout the kingdom. The principal nobility made a tender of their services to their Sovereign: and some of them received commissions to levy regiments towards the suppression of the rebellion. Bodies of volunteers were incorporated in London, and in many other places; associations were formed; and large contributions were raised in different towns, counties, and communities. *The merchants of London alone, resolved to raise* TWO REGIMENTS AT THEIR OWN EXPENCE. They, besides, agreed to support the public credit, by receiving, as usual, bank notes in payment, for the purposes of traffic; and the friends of the constitution were encouraged, animated, and confirmed in their principles, by *several spirited productions published at that period.*

THE Parliament met in October; and both Houses were most cordial in their addresses, to support the illustrious House of Hanover, and the constitution of 1688. The *Habeas Corpus* act was SUSPENDED, *and several persons were apprehended on suspicion of* TREASONABLE PRACTICES. The trained bands of London were reviewed by his Majesty. The county regiments were completed. *The volunteers in different parts of the kingdom, employed themselves industriously in the exercise of arms*; and the whole nation seemed to rise up as one man against popery and slavery.

THE Pretender received considerable supplies of money, artillery, and provisions, by single ships that arrived from France, where his interest seemed to rise in proportion to his success; but the French made no attempts at an invasion. Government, however, to be prepared against such an event, appointed Admiral Vernon to command a squadron in the Downes, to observe the motions of the enemy by sea, especially in the harbours of Dunkirk and Boulogne; and his cruisers took several ships loaded with soldiers, officers, and amunition, destined for the service of the Pretender.

WHEN he had unaccountably advanced within an hundred miles of the capital, it was filled with terror and confusion. Orders were given for forming a camp on *Finchley Common.*

Common, where THE KING *refolved to take the field in perfon.* Some priests were apprehended. The militia of London were kept in readiness to march. Double watches were posted at the city gates, and signals of alarm appointed. The city volunteers were incorporated into a regiment. The practitioners of the law, headed by the judges, engaged in military affociations. Other communities followed their example. Even the managers of the theatres offered to raife a body of their dependants, for the fervice of the country. Notwithstanding all this preparation, the Jacobites, as the rebels advanced into England, were elevated to an infolence of hope, which they were at no pains to conceal. They formed intrigues, to miflead, to corrupt, and to arm. Some weak and infatuated people were led into the fnare; while others, who had neither honour, nor partiotifm, nor property to lofe, hoping fome acquifition from the general convulfion, waited with the moft calm indifference the iffue of this important crifis.

But fhort was the duration of this ftate of fufpence. The golden dreams of the young Pretender foon vanifhed. He had now advanced into the middle of the kingdom, and except a few that joined him at Manchefter, a place long noted for reftleffnefs and difaffection, not a foul appeared in his behalf. This was owing to the good fenfe of the nation, and the falutary, though tardy fteps of its mild government. It appeared as if all the Jacobites of England had been annihilated at once. As for the Pretender, after retreating with great rapidity into the north of Scotland, he was totally routed by the Duke of Cumberland, at the battle of Culloden; and the kingdom once more faved from flavery, from bigotry, and from ruin.

OF THE MENACED INVASIONS, IN 1755, 1756, 1758, AND 1759.

THE peace of Aix-la-Chapelle, in 1748, soon appeared on the part of France, to be insincere; and was made for no other purpose, by that treacherous nation, than to gain a little time, the more effectually to accomplish their ends. Their aim was to confine the British subjects in North America, to the coasts only; and for that purpose, they made encroachments, built forts within our territories, entered into secret alliances and intrigues with the Indian tribes; and sent troops at different times from France to Canada, under various pretences, but in effect to be prepared at a future period openly to enforce their designs.

BUT the vanity and overweening confidence of the French, never easily restrained within moderate bounds, prompted them to commence hostilities, before they had sufficient power to maintain their depredations. Their attack and defeat of young Washington, now president of America, and likewise of the old and the obstinate General Braddock, were deemed, by the British court, and the voice of the nation, a sufficient breach of the peace; and after retaliating, by taking a great number of French merchantmen, and some thousands of their seamen, war was declared against France.

ENGLAND had a fleet, at this time, able to combat all the maritime powers in Europe. It consisted of 6 ships of 100 guns and upwards—13 of 90—8 of 80—5 of 74—20 of 70—4 of 66—1 of 64—33 of 60—3 of 54—28 of 50—4 of 44—30 of 40—42 of 20—besides many sloops, bomb ketches,

fire

fire ships and tenders; whereas, the whole French navy including those on the stocks, were only 9 of 80 guns—21 of 74—1 of 72—4 of 70—31 of 64—2 of 60—6 of 50—and 32 frigates.

Among the many projects of France, before war was declared, was the old one of an invasion. The French made no scruple of owning in 1755, that they intended to make a powerful invasion on Great Britain, early in the following spring. But as the nation knew the inferiority of their marine force, it did not excite much alarm, although the report of the invasion daily increasing, in the begining of the year 1756, some steps were taken to increase our internal defence.

France, mean while, began to repair and fortify Dunkirk. She employed great numbers of artificers and seamen, in equipping a formidable squadron of ships, at Brest; and assembling a strong body of land forces, as well as a considerable number of transports, really threatened the island of Great Britain with a dangerous invasion.

The nation began now to be seized with consternation. The apprehensions and distractions of the kingdom increased, as they had not a sufficient military force, while the militia had been much neglected. The perplexed and alarming situation of the country, at this juncture, plainly evinced the expediency of such a national force; although different parties were divided about the nature of such a provision.

Some of the warmest friends of the nation, proposed a well regulated militia, as an institution that would effectually answer the purpose of defending a wide extended seacoast from invasion; while, on the other hand, this proposal was ridiculed and represented as impracticable or useless, by some then in power, *so totaly different in their policy,* in this respect, from the present ABLE and PATRIOTIC ADMINISTRATION, those zealous promoters of a POWERFUL and WELL DISCIPLINED MILITIA; and it was scouted besides by all the officers of the army. Mean while, as the experiment could not be immediately tried, and the present juncture demanded some instant determination, recourse was had to a foreign aid.

The king, about the end of March, sent a message to parliament, informing them, that he had received repeated advices from different persons and places, that a design had been formed by the French court to invade England, or Ireland; and the great preparations of forces, ships, artillery, and warlike stores, then notoriously making in the ports of France, opposite to the British coast; together with the language of the French ministers in some foreign courts, left little room to doubt the reality of such a design: that his majesty had augmented his forces, both by sea and land, and taken proper measures and precautions for putting his kingdom in a posture of defence. He added, that in order further to strengthen the country, he had made a requisition of a body of Hessian troops. To this, both houses returned the most warm and affectionate addresses.

But the terrors of the nation, demanded some more foreign aid. Twelve battalions of Hanoverians, with a detachment of artillery, were sent for; and such expedition was used, that in the course of the ensuing month both Hessians and Hanoverians arrived in England, and encamped in different parts of the kingdom.

The invading armament of the French, however, which engrossed the attention of the British nation, was merely a feint, to cover the real intention of these preparations for the capture of Minorca, which succeeded according to their most sanguine wishes.

A PRO-

A proclamation had been issued, too, to prevent the enemy receiving any supplies of cattle, in case of their landing. It required that all officers, civil and military, upon the first appearance of any hostile attempt to land upon the coasts of the kingdom, should immediately cause all horses, oxen, and cattle, which might be fit for draught or burthen, and not actually employed in the King's service, or in the defence of the country: and also, so far as might be practicable, all other cattle and provisions to be driven, and removed twenty miles at least, from the place where such hostile attempt should be made, and to secure the same, so as that they might not fall into the hands or power of those, who should make such attempt; regard being had, however, that the respective owners should suffer as little damage, as might be consistent with the public safety.

But the fear of an invasion for that year, having subsided, when the real object of their preparations, Minorca, was fatally ascertained, the auxiliaries of his Majesty's electoral dominions were ordered home, and the Hessians some time after followed them.

The parliament met in December, which the King opened with a speech, wherein he recommended, among other matters, that which had been much neglected of late, a due attention to the militia. For this end, *he left to the care and diligence of parliament, the forming of* A NATIONAL MILITIA, *planned and regulated with equal regard to the just rights of his crown and people; an institution which might become our great resource, in times of general danger.* The militia was accordingly next year, by an act of parliament, put on an excellent footing, and since very much improved.

As there was great reason still to fear that the French would invade this kingdom, and as it was necessary that great part of our regular forces should be employed abroad, so the militia bill was brought into parliament on an extensive and useful plan. This was such a constitutional measure as afforded great pleasure and satisfaction to the nation in general; *and yet some discontented and factious persons, as in the late militia bill of Ireland, so loudly exclaimed against it, that many of the people, particularly in Yorkshire, actually rose in a body, and demolished the house where the Justices of the peace and deputy Lieutenants had met, to make choice of such as were to serve.*

OF THE MENACED INVASION OF 1758, AND 1759, BY FRANCE.

The French ministry, in the year 1758, practiced every stratagem in order to supply Canada with troops, artillery, stores, and ammunition for its defence, against the operations of the British forces, which greatly outnumbered the French upon that Continent. To elude the vigilance of the English cruisers, they detached the ships destined for America, both single and in convoys, sometimes from the Mediterranean, sometimes from their harbours, in the Channel.

They assembled transports in one part, in order to withdraw the attention of their enemies from another, where their convoys lay ready for sailing; and in boisterous weather, when the English could no longer block up their harbours,

harbours, which they did with confiderable effect, their ftorefhips came forth, and hazarded the voyage, for the relief of their American fettlements.

Although the navy of France was by this time fo reduced, that it could neither face the Englifh at fea, nor furnifh proper convoys for their commerce, her miniftry neverthelefs attempted to alarm the fubjects of Great Britain, with the old project of an invafion.

Flat-bottomed boats were built, tranfports collected, large fhips of the line equipped, and troops ordered to affemble on the coaft for embarkation. This, however, was no more than a fcheme to aroufe the apprehenfions of the Englifh, difconcert the adminiftration, prejudice the national credit, and deter the government from fending forces to keep alive the war in Germany.

This year a Dr. Henfey, an obfcure phyfician, whofe brother was fecretary to the Spanifh ambaffador at the Hague, was apprehended for treafonable practices, and found guilty in the court of King's Bench, on an indictment for high treafon. He was convicted among other things, of having given intelligence to the French court, through the means of his brother, of the failing and deftination of every fquadron and armament; and he had advifed an invafion of Great Britain, at a certain time and place, as the moft effectual method of diftreffing the government, throwing the nation into confufion, and affecting the public credit. His life was, however, faved, owing to fome material difcovery that it was reported he made to government; and he was pardoned, on condition of going into perpetual exile.

Whether it was from defpair that the French in 1759, really formed a plan for the invafion of Great Britain,

and

and Ireland, is uncertain; but surely no other motive could have impelled them in making one great effort to convulse this country, at a period when their navy was so reduced, and their coasts so harrassed by the English, as they had experienced the preceding year.

NOTWITHSTANDING the disasters of France, her ministry now persisted in a serious design of invasion. They prepared a considerable fleet at Rochfort, Brest, and Port Louis, to be commanded by Monf. de Conflans, and reinforced by a considerable body of troops, which were actually assembled under the Duc d'Aiguillion, at Vannes, in Lower Bretagne. Flat-bottomed boats to be used in this expedition, were prepared in different ports on the coast of France; and a small squadron was equipped at Dunkirk, under the command of an enterprizing adventurer called Thurot.

IN the latter end of May, the King sent a message to both Houses, acquainting them, that he had received advices of preparations making by the French court, with a design to invade Great Britain; that though persuaded by the universal zeal and affection of his people, any such attempt must, under the blessing of God, end in the destruction of those who engaged in it; yet he apprehended he should not act consistent with that paternal care and concern which he had always shewn for the safety and preservation of his subjects, if he omitted any means in his power that might be necessary for their defence; he therefore acquainted the parliament with his having received repeated intelligence of the enemy's preparations; to the end, that his Majesty might, if he should think proper, in pursuance of the late militia act, cause the militia, or such part thereof as should be necessary, to be drawn out and embodied, in order to march as occasion should require.

No sooner was the message read in both houses, than each seperately resolved to present a most loyal address; wherein they assured his Majesty, that they would support him against all attempts whatever, with their lives and fortunes. The Commons requested, that his Majesty would give directions to his lieutenants of the several counties, ridings, and places, within South Britain, to use their utmost diligence and attention, in executing the several acts of parliament, made for the better ordering of the militia.

These, and other precautionary steps, were accordingly taken. But the administration, of which the illustrious father of our present admirable minister, the late Lord Chatham, was the life and soul, placed their chief dependance upon the strength of the navy. Being apprized of all these particulars, they took such measures to defeat the purposed invasion, as must have conveyed a very high idea of the power of Great Britain, to those who considered that, exclusive of the force opposed to this design, she, at the same time, carried on the most vigorous and important operations of the war in Germany, America, and the East and West Indies.

Thurot's armament at Dunkirk, was watched by an English squadron in the Downes; and he was afterwards defeated and slain by Captain Elliot, in a descent on Ireland. The Port of Havre was guarded by Admiral Rodney. Mr. Boscawen had been stationed off Toulon, of which fleet he took three ships of 74 guns each, burnt one of 80, and another of 74 guns, in his defeat of Monf. de la Clue, when he had failed to form a junction with the Brest fleet. The coast of Vannes was scoured by a small squadron, under the command of Captain Duff, detached from Sir Edward Hawke, who had, during the whole summer, blocked up the harbour of Brest, where the French admiral, M. de Conflans, lay with his fleet, in order to be

joined

joined by the other divisions of the armament. These different squadrons of the British navy, were connected by a a chain of separate cruisers; so that the whole coast of France, from Dunkirk to the extremity of Bretagne, were distressed by an actual blockade.

ADMIRAL Rodney, in order to prevent the flat-bottomed boats at Havre de Grace from joining the fleet, and thus frustrate the whole scheme of the invasion, attacked the town with two vessels, and threw such a number of bombs into it, that most of their magazines were destroyed. The bombardment continued fifty hours without intermission, and was so dreadful, that the town was three times set on fire. The flat-bottomed boats were likewise set on fire, and continued burning six hours, and took several hundred men to extinguish it. The conduct of Rodney, on this occasion, struck such a terror into the French ministry, that they became divided in their councils; *for they found it* ALMOST IMPOSSIBLE *that they could* INVADE BRITAIN, WHILE HER NAVY DID THEIR DUTY.

THE French ministry being thus hampered, forbore their attempt upon Britain; and the projected invasion seemed to hang in suspence till the month of August, in the beginning of which their army in Germany was defeated at Minden. Their designs in that country being baffled by this disaster, they seemed to convert their chief attention to their sea-armament; the preparations were resumed with redoubled vigour; and even after the defeat of La Clue, they resolved to try their fortune in a descent. They now proposed to disembark a body of troops in Ireland. Thurot received orders to sail from Dunkirk with the first opportunity, and shape his course round the northern parts of Scotland, that he might alarm the coast of Ireland, and make a diversion from that part where Conflans intended to effectuate the disembarkation of his forces.

The

The transports and ships of war were assembled at Brest and Rochfort, having on board a train of artillery, with saddles and other accoutrements for cavalry, to be mounted in Ireland. A body of French troops, including part of the Irish brigade, was kept in readiness to embark; and the young Pretender having agreed to certain terms, proposed by France, remained in the neighbourhood of Vannes incognito, in order once more to hazard his person, and countenance a revolt in the dominions of Great Britain.

The execution of this scheme was, however, prevented by the vigilance of Sir Edward Hawke, who blocked up the harbour of Brest, with a fleet of twenty three capital ships; while another squadron of smaller ships, and frigates, under the command of Captain Duff, continued to cruise along the French coast, from Port l'Orient, in Bretagne, to the Point of St. Gilles, in Poitou. At length, however, in the beginning of November, the British squadron, commanded by Sir Edward Hawke, Sir Charles Hardy, and Rear-Admiral Geary, were driven from the coast of France by stress of weather; and, on the ninth day of the month, anchored in Torbay.

The French admiral, Conflans, snatched this opportunity of sailing from Brest, with twenty-one sail of the line, and four frigates, in hopes of being able to destroy the English squadron, commanded by Captain Duff, before the larger fleet could return from the coast of England. Sir Edward Hawke, having received intelligence that the French fleet had sailed from Brest, immediately stood to sea, in order to pursue them; and, *in the mean time, the government issued orders for guarding all those parts of the coast, that were thought the most exposed to an invasion. The land forces were put in motion, and quartered along the shore, in Kent and Sussex; all the ships of war, in the different harbours, even those that had just arrived from America, were ordered to put to sea, and every step was taken to disconcert the designs of the enemy.*

While these measures were taken with equal vigour and deliberation, Sir Edward Hawke steered his course directly for Quiberon, on the coast of Bretagne, which he supposed would be the rendezvous of the French squadron: but notwithstanding his utmost efforts, he was driven, by a hard gale, considerably to the westward, where he was joined by two frigates, the Maidstone and Coventry. These he directed to keep a head of the squadron. The weather growing more moderate, the former, made the signal for seeing a fleet on the twentieth day of November, at half past eight in the morning, and in an hour afterwards discovered them to be the enemy's squadron. They were at that time in chace of Captain Duff's squadron, which now joined the large fleet, after having run some risque of being taken.

Sir Edward Hawke, who, when the Maidstone gave the first notice, had formed the line a-breast, now perceiving that the French admiral endeavoured to escape, with all the sail he could carry, threw out a signal for seven of his ships, that were nearest the enemy, to chace; and endeavour to detain them, until they could be reinforced by the rest of the squadron, which were ordered to form into a line of battle, a-head, as they chaced, that no time might be lost in the pursuit.

Considering the roughness of the weather, which was extremely tempestuous; the nature of the coast, which is in this place rendered very hazardous, by a great number of sand-banks, shoals, rocks, and islands, as entirely unknown to the British sailors, as they were familiar to the French navigators; the dangers of a short day, dark night, and lee-shore; it required extraordinary resolution in the

English

English admiral, to attempt hostilities on this occasion; but Sir Edward Hawke, steeled with the integrity and fortitude of his own heart, *animated by a warm love for his country; and well acquainted with the importance of the stake on which the safety of that country, in a great measure, depended, was resolved to run extraordinary risques, in his endeavours to frustrate, at once, a boasted scheme, projected for the annoyance of his fellow subjects.*

With respect to his ships of the line, he had but the advantage of one, in point of number, and no superiority in men or metal; consequently, Mr. de Conflans might have hazarded a fair battle, on the open sea, without any imputation of temerity; but he thought proper to play a more artful game, though it did not succeed according to his expectations. He kept his fleet in a body, and retired close in shore, with a view to draw the English squadron among the shoals and islands; on which, he hoped, they would pay dear for their rashness and impetuosity; while he and his officers, who were perfectly acquainted with the navigation, could either stay, and take advantage of the disaster; or, if hard pressed, retire through channels, unknown to the British pilots.

At half an hour after two, the van of the English fleet began the engagement, with the rear of the enemy, in the neighbourhood of Belleisle. Every ship, as she advanced, poured in a broadside on the sternmost of the French, and bore down upon their van, leaving the rear to those that came after. Sir Edward Hawke, in the Royal George, of one hundred and ten guns, reserved his fire, in passing through the rear of the enemy; and ordered his master to bring him along side of the French admiral, who commanded in person, on board of the Soleil Royal, a ship mounted with eighty cannon, and provided with a compliment of 1,200 men.

1,200 men. When the pilot remonstrated, that he could not obey his command, without the most imminent risque of running upon a shoal, the brave veteran replied "*you have done your duty in shewing me the danger; now you are to comply with my order, and lay me along side of the Soleil Royal.*"

His wish was gratified. The Royal George ranged up with the French admiral. The Thesée, another large ship of the enemy, running up between the two commanders, sustained the fire that was reserved for the Soleil Royal, but, in returning the first broadside, in consequence of the high sea that entered her lower deck-ports, and filled her with water, she went to the bottom. Notwithstanding the boisterous weather, a great number of ships, on both sides, fought with equal fury and dubious success, till about four in the afternoon, when the Formidable struck her colours. The Superbe shared the fate of the Thesée, in going to the bottom. The Heros hauled down her colours, in token of submission, and dropped anchor; but the wind was so high, that no boat could be sent to take possession. By this time, day-light began to fail, and the greater part of the French fleet escaped, under cover of the darkness.

Night approaching, the wind blowing with augmented violence, on a lee shore, and the British squadron being entangled among unknown shoals and islands; Sir Edward Hawke made the signal for anchoring to the westward, of the small island Dumat; and here the fleet remained all night, in a very dangerous riding, alarmed by the fury of the storm, and the incessant firing of guns of distress, without knowing whether it proceeded from friend or enemy. The Soleil Royal had, under favour of the night, anchored also in the midst of the British squadron; but at day-break, Mr. de Conflans ordered her cable to be cut, and she drove ashore to the westward of Crozic.

The

The English admiral immediately made signal to the Essex, to slip cable and pursue her; and in obeying this order, she ran unfortunately on a sand bank called Le Four, where another ship of the British squadron, was already grounded. Here they were both irrecoverably lost, in spite of all the assistance that could be given; but all their men and part of their stores were saved; and the wreck set on fire, by order of the admiral.

He likewise detached the Portland, Chatham, and Vengeance, to destroy the Soleil Royal, which was burned by her own people, before the English ships could approach; but they arrived time enough to reduce the Heros to ashes on the Le Four, where she had also been stranded; and the Juste, another of their great ships, perished in the mouth of the Loire.

The Admiral, preceiving seven large ships of the enemy riding at anchor between point Penves and the mouth of the river Vilaine, made the signal to weigh, in order to attack them; but the fury of the storm increased to such a a degree, that he was obliged to remain at anchor, and even ordered the top-gallant masts to be struck.

In the mean time the French ships, being lightened of their cannon, their officers took advantage of the flood, and a more moderate gale, under the land, to enter the Vilaine, where they lay within half a mile of the entrance, protected by some occasional batteries erected on the shore, and by two large frigates, moored across the mouth of the harbour. Thus they were effectually secured from any attempts of small vessels; and as for large ships, there was not water sufficient to float them within fighting distance of the enemy.

On

On the whole, this battle in which a very inconsiderable number of lives were lost, may be considered *as one of the most perilous and important actions that ever happened in any war between the two nations;* for it not only gave the finishing blow to the naval powers of France, which was totally disabled from undertaking any thing of consequence during that war; but consequently *defeated totally the* PROJECTED INVASION, *which had hung so long over the apprehensions of Great Britain.*

CHAP.

CHAP. XV.

OF THE PREPARATIONS IN 1779, AND 1782, AGAINST INVASION.

WE approach now an interesting period, when the unwary policy of Lewis XVI. sowed the seeds of his own destruction. He did not perceive, that by treacherously exciting an ungrateful child, to throw off all allegiance to her tender and fostering parent; that he was steeling the heart of France, against every tie of affection and duty. For it was by no means from any regard to the liberties of mankind, that Lewis unsheathed the sword in the cause of illiberal America; but for the pernicious love of universal dominion. The slavery of the human race, has been always the darling aim of insiduous France. This is still the case. Her monarchy would formerly have bound mankind in cords of silk; her anarchy would now fetter them in chains of iron.

But when intrigues of France with America were discovered, the country was soon put in a state of defence, against another menaced invasion. Although the combined fleets appeared off Plymouth, in autumn, 1779, they studiously avoided our land batteries, and never came to anchor. It however so far alarmed the country, as they were 6c sail of the line, and 20 frigates, besides transports, that the moſt vigorous meaſures were adopted to render any attempt abortive.

THE parliament met in November. His Majeſty graciouſly acquainted them, that " though the deſigns and attempts of
" our enemies to invade this kingdom, by the bleſſing of
" providence, had been hitherto fruſtrated and diſappointed,
" *They ſtill menace us with great armaments and preparations;*
" *but we are, I truſt, on our part well prepared to meet every*
" *attack, and repel every inſult. I know the character of my*
" *brave people. The menaces of their enemies, and the ap-*
" *proach of danger, have no other effect on their minds, but to*
" *animate their courage, and to call forth that national ſpirit,*
" *which has ſo often checked, and defeated, the projects of* AM-
" BITION *and* INJUSTICE *; and enabled the Britiſh fleets and*
" *armies to* PROTECT THEIR OWN COUNTRY *; to vindicate*
" THEIR OWN RIGHTS *; and, at the ſame time, to uphold and*
" PRESERVE THE LIBERTIES OF EUROPE, *from the* RESTLESS
" *and* INCROACHING POWER *of the Houſe of Bourbon.*

" I HAVE great ſatisfaction in renewing the aſſurances of
" my entire approbation of the *good conduct and diſcipline*
" *of the* MILITIA, *and of their ſteady perſeverance in their*
" DUTY *: And I return my cordial thanks to all ranks of my*
" *loyal ſubjects, who have ſtood forth in this arduous con-*
" *juncture :* and by their *zeal,* their *influence,* and their *per-*
" *ſonal ſervice,* have given *confidence,* as well as *ſtrength* to
" the *National defence.*

HAD the combined fleets, at that time, met with the Britiſh, as they were ſo very inferior, and have forced them into an action, the conſequences probably would have been fatal. In that caſe, France would have immediately invaded this country with a formidable body of troops, as every thing was prepared for their embarkation. But the prudence of avoiding an action, when there was no proſpect

pect of success, and great hazard of a defeat, prevented a powerful descent on our coast, and saved us much blood and treasure.

It would have been a very dangerous enterprize to have invaded England, while our fleet was entire, although it was far inferior to the combined fleets of France and Spain; for, as the accidents of wind and weather would have prevented such a great fleet from keeping together for any length of time, and consequently cut off greatly the communication with the army which they might have possibly landed; our fleet, meanwhile could have intercepted their convoys, blocked up the harbour where their magazines were established, and their forces must soon have perished. For it is not sufficient that the enemy debarks an army; it must be continually supplied and protected from France; otherwise, however numerous, it cannot make any progress, or penetrate into the kingdom.

It is needless to record any more steps taken by government, against invasion, in the years 1778, 1779, and 1782, further than to observe that volunteer corps were set on foot by subscription, to aid the land forces, and every other measure was adopted that could strengthen the kingdom.

From the foregoing history, some material points may be deduced, in cases of invasion, which are highly necessary to reflect on at this moment. We may observe from it, that the invaders have been generally invited to such attempts, by *traitors* in the bosom of this country: and that we have

been

been likewise, very much indebted to *storms*, for the dispersion of the fleets of the enemy, and by that means for the failure of their enterprizes.

Now as we are pretty certain that several persons of the above description are in the country, and that by the suspension of the Habeas Corpus act, it is to be hoped that their seditious designs will all be defeated; yet as we must not trust too much to the friendship of tempests, we cannot be too diligent in arming, in vigilance, and in the strictness of military discipline.

If we continue firm and united, the constitution is safe, even from the sting of any political scorpion. And as to the democratic tyranny in France, it is fast dissolving. Traitor destroys traitor; and regicide destroys regicide. But though the treason against society, seems to increase with every succeeding butchery of the minor faction of the day, yet it is by those terrible means only, that society itself is beginning to awake from its delirium, and to resume its substantial rights, and its former order. For soon must the mind be purified by this horrid and sanguinary fermentation.

END OF THE HISTORY.

CHAP.

CHAP. XVI.

A VIEW OF THE PRESENT STATE OF AFFAIRS.

AMONG the various convulsions that have happened to the human race, the present is the most formidable and tremendous. It seems to be a hurricane of the mind, tearing up by the roots all the tender and philanthropic faculties of the soul; all the refinements of the sciences and the arts; all the soft and reciprocal endearments that make life desirous, and society preferable to the unbounded freedom of brutal ferocity. The destructive hand of pseudo-philosophic civility is rapidly extirpating all civilization. And were not this wide-wasting havock soon stopt in its career, the mind of man would be a wilderness of barbarism, and the face of the earth one dreary savage waste.

In the humane and glorious task of destroying this sanguinary and ruinous system, Britain appears towering among the nations. And if ever she stood greater at any period than another, it is now, when, with gigantic might, she is combating not only to preserve her own freedom, but the liberty of mankind.

To effect these indispensible objects, the nation is almost unanimous. If we investigate the public mind throughout the empire, there is but one opinion about the necessity and the justice of the war. However some individuals may lament, and a few disaffected people may croak about the temporary inconveniencies attending it, yet all the real friends of their king and country, agree as to its being continued with ardour, until we can secure a peace, that shall not endanger the FUTURE SAFETY OF THE CONSTITUTION.

If we look into parliament, we perceive the utmost unanimity. *Never was there such an* UNINFLUENCED *and* INDEPENDENT MAJORITY *possessed by* ANY ADMINISTRATION. All that was estimable among opposition, in point of solid virtue, and true patriotism, have fled with horror from their former associates, when their views were discovered; and cordially given their support to the present mild, but firm, and spirited men, that so ably conduct the public affairs. Nothing is left of an opposition, but the gross republican dregs of whiggism. Such a motley, visionary, group of irascible, and desperate politicians, never existed in parliament since the days of Cromwell. But as there are among them men of great talents, they cannot be too narrowly watched. For, though weak in number, they are strong in the depth of plan, and the malignity of design. Their aim is not so much to impress parliament, as to mislead the people. If their harangues be but read with avidity without doors, and make the least impression on the million, it is the chief end of their oratory; for they rely on *time* to carry their plans into effect. They are but too well aware that almost every man who has the least property at stake, can never listen but with detestation, to the syren tongues of such worshippers of French Reform. To those meek preachers of treacherous peace, internal tranquillity is but the rock of their despair, and on the quick sands of commotion, rests their anchor of hope. They cannot smile, but in anarchy's success; and, when they look grave, Britain is sure to be victorious.

Perceiving that all their insidious schemes, for altering that Constitution which they pretend so much to revere, were scouted by the real body of the people, as much as their virulent invectives against the war with their friends, the anarchists, they have adopted this sessions a new plan. Under pretext of supporting the Constitution as it is, until they have an opportunity to reform it as they please, they

endeavour

endeavour to praise an excellence which they secretly decry, in order to secure a reputation, by which that very excellence may be the more completely undermined.

Their diabolical aim, of late, has been to distract, depress, and disarm the country. They have systematically defended the ringleaders of sedition: they have assailed the militia, that increasing bulwark of constitutional defence; and they have reviled all alliance for mutual protection. They have poured forth the most acrimonious slander against those who, preferring the safety of their country, to their pernicious doctrines, discarded their friendship, with every mark of astonishment and detestation; and renounced all commerce with such WHIG APOSTATES, when they discovered their *latent* intentions. They have attacked the conduct of the war, being so repeatedly defeated as to its principle, with all the arrogance of malevolence, and all the virulence of disappointment and chagrin. Victory, to them is defeat; and defeat, victory.

They have stiled free gifts for constitutional safety, compulsory benevolences for national destruction. They have endeavoured to punish men in office, for their voluntary subscriptions, by oppressing them with a partial and unproductive taxation. They have croaked about the distresses of the poor, yet they wished to have added to their burthen, by opposing all exclusive self-taxing of the rich. They have distributed hand-bills to palsy constitutional defence; and have declaimed against those that were circulated to strengthen the public force. They have trampled upon all precedent, when their destructive reform was the topic; and they have never clung to it, but when their commentaries, upon precedent, if followed, would have equally promoted the general ruin. They have boasted of subscribing to support a foreign constitution; while they have audaciously gloried in with-holding all voluntary aid, in the hour

of

of peril, from that very conſtitution which ſo admirably ſupports them. They have never, indeed, made one motion to arm the country; but on the contrary, all their motions have tended to enfeeble it; and to impede the public buſineſs.

VOLUNTARY SUBSCRIPTIONS.

As to the ſubject of voluntary ſubſcriptions, in point of their legality, which has been lately a great topic of diſcourſe, we cannot reſiſt obſerving, that Mr. Fox, having been violently againſt that meaſure, it is but juſt to ſhew his inconſiſtency, as to his opinions of ſuch ſubſcriptions, when he was *in*, and when he was *out* of office. In the beginning of 1778, during Lord North's adminiſtration, when volunteer ſubſcriptions were ſet on foot, Mr. Fox being then *out of place*, he declaimed vehemently againſt them; and treated Scotland and Mancheſter with much acrimony, becauſe they were ſo zealous on that occaſion.

In 1782, when Mr. Fox was *in place*, ſimilar ſteps being taken to guard the kingdom, he defended the meaſure which he had formerly reprobated. He ſaid, in vindication of it, " that neceſſity gave riſe to new reſources; and the moſt " natural reſource the people could have, was, to arm them-" ſelves in their own defence." He afterwards remarked, " that if the country had been armed, the *riots*, in 1780, " would have been ſuppreſſed in the firſt inſtance. In Ire-" land the volunteers had ſuppreſſed all rioters and *com-* " *binations*. Theſe volunteers had aſſociated to preſerve " their rights, and had preſerved regularity and diſcipline; " which proved how ſafe it was to entruſt arms in the hands " of the people. At preſent there could be but one opinion " with regard to England, and that was to put her in an " immediate ſtate of defence."

MR.

Mr. Fox, in 1794, being *again out of place*, decried his former doctrine of 1782, and naturally adopted that of 1778; by supporting a motion, "That it is *a dangerous* "and *unconstitutional* mode for the government to solicit "aid from the people, either as a gift, grant, loan, bene-"volence, or contribution."

Whether it be that the opposition are *afraid of* the kingdom being put into an excellent posture of defence, is unfair, although not difficult, perhaps, to determine. But surely no real friend to the Constitution, can deem it dangerous for government "to arm the people in their "own defence," *according to Mr. Fox's doctrine*, for the year 1782, "as the most natural resource," when Britain is threatened with an invasion from France.

As to its *legality*, if it has not been indisputable, it has been proved to be incontrovertable. *Free gifts were always legal.*

Lord Coke says, "If the subjects, *of their free will,* "*without any compulsion,* give to the King, for public "uses, any sums of money, this is not prohibited by "statute."

The petition of right declares, "That no man can "be hereafter *compelled* to make, or yield, any gift, &c. "without common consent, by act of parliament." This evidently alludes to *compulsory* gifts; but does it *prevent the subject from subscribing, of his own free will, to secure his liberty and property?*

In the year 1745, a committee was chosen for the disposal of the *subscription money*, at Guildhall, London, consisting of the Lord Mayor, the Aldermen, their Deputies, the Wardens of Companies, the City Chamberlain, the Master of the Rolls, the Twelve Judges, &c.—Could

ALL

ALL THESE GREAT OFFICIAL CHARACTERS be *united* for the purpose of doing an ILLEGAL ACT?

BESIDES this, Lord Hardwicke said, of those voluntary aids of 1745, that " Men of property, of all ranks, crowd-
" ed in with *liberal* subscriptions, beyond the examples of
" former times, and *uncompelled* by any law; and yet in
" the most *legal* and *warrantable* manner."

INDEED, it is highly ludicrous to reflect upon the affair of subscriptions, that those men who endeavoured to revile parliamentary representation the most, have been very vociferous in their declamations, against any *out-door* aid being given towards THE SUPPORT OF THE CONSTITUTION! *But had similar aids been raised by certain clubs, for certain purposes, would they have objected to the mode of self-taxation, now adopted by the liberal and the affluent?*

As to Lord Shelburne's volunteer plan of 1782, upon which opposition quibbled so much; after his Lordship had suspended the public mind, for some time, upon his meaning, he had better have remained in silence, than have said, that, " By the plan of 1782, the officers were
" to have been appointed by THE PEOPLE: but in this,
" they were to be nominated by THE CROWN."

WHATEVER was his Lordship's meaning, in 1782; yet so explaining it, in 1794, with the destruction of France before his eyes, owing chiefly to the establishing of two distinct military powers; the censorious will be ill-natured enough to explain it not much to his Lordship's advantage; especially when they recollect that his now coy political lover, Mr. Fox, stiled him in that year, when they quarrelled about the jockeyship of power " as a *giant* in promises, but a *pigmy* in performances; as a man, not of a description to command that *faith* and *trust* which, in a great predicament, was indispensible."

MR.

Mr. Pitt very properly and elegantly obferved, upon this bufinefs, that "an act merely *voluntary*, having *the* *fanction of* PARLIAMENT, mixed the *zeal* and *warmth* of INDIVIDUAL WILL with the power of LEGAL AUTHORITY, and gave an *energy* which NO LAW could do. What was fo likely, he added, to put an end to the invading menaces of France, as to fee INDIVIDUAL EXERTION *fuccouring* and *outrunning* the VOICE and EFFORTS of PARLIAMENT."

SUSPENSION OF THE HABEAS CORPUS ACT.

WHEN this act was about being fufpended by parliament, to check all Jacobin reforms, the oppofition clamour to it was unbounded. If they have ridiculed all alarm hitherto, at our liberties being in danger, they are now become very great alarmifts indeed, about liberties of a more partial nature. *But the* INNOCENT *need not be under any dread.* For if there be any fault in the executive power, it is in having fhewn too much tardinefs, and too much lenity, in their coercive meafures.

THE fufpending of the Habeas Corpus Act, duly confidered, is a ftep, at this moment, very falutary and proper. Its fufpenfion is not owing to the executive power, or to parliament, but to CERTAIN CLUBS and CERTAIN SOCIETIES, whofe *machinations* rendered it abfolutely neceffary; for, if that act were not fufpended, in the hour of *glaring confpiracy*, we fhou'd foon have NO ACTS TO ENFORCE!

OF what avail would be our juftly boafted Conftitution, were there not a power lodged in the bofom of parliament, to inveft the executive government, upon extraordinary occafions, like the prefent, with fuch an ample and *refponfible* authority, *as may enfure the prefervation of that Conftitution?* If there be no power, in a moment of peril which menaces the deftruction of THAT ACT, and of ALL

ACTS, to IMPRISON A CRIMINAL FEW, that we may thereby SECURE THE LIBERTY OF THE INNOCENT MANY, the *Habeas Corpus Act* would become that very instrument and cause of our slavery and ruin, which it was intended to prevent.

HAD government been culpably delicate or timid, in acquainting parliament with the pending danger, till commotion and carnage had ensued, it would have been then very properly asked,

WHY was not this act suspended, that the persons of *some* might be confined, in order that the persons of *all* had not been endangered by *that liberty* which CONSPIRATORS enjoy, *merely by virtue of this act?*

WHY did not those who knew of these conspirators, and who were to guard us against them, at least *confine them where they could do no mischief?*

THE only answer must have been this: Because they had NO POWER, by LAW, to do it.

WHY then, the next question would be, did they not *ask*, and *demand* it, of PARLIAMENT?

To this it would have been answered,—Because they had too great a veneration for the *Habeas Corpus act*, the idol and defence of the nation:

THE general voice would have then exclaimed;

WHY do you tell us of our idol and our Defence? Call it no longer by these names. It is our *poison* and our *ruin:* if a fatal veneration for the *Habeas Corpus act*, has brought destruction upon us, and prevented the measures which alone could have saved us. We are *now* DEAD *for fear of* DEATH!

DEATH! *And we have* LOST THIS ACT, *and* ALL THE EF-
FECTS *of it,* FOR EVER, *out of a superstitious dread of suffering* TRAITORS *to lose the benefit of it* FOR A SEASON!

SUCH would have been the natural and indignant re-
flections in every patriotic bosom, had the executive power
neglected to have laid the state of the nation before parliament, as to the conspiracy against the Constitution; and
not have moved, in consequence, for the suspension of
that act.

IT is proper here to observe, that although it has been
suspended *nine* times since the Revolution, it has never
afforded matter for *one complaint*. And this is not at all
wonderful, when it is considered as a step which every
administration have been compelled to adopt, with the utmost reluctance. For in the execution of that ungracious,
though necessary task, none can feel more uneasiness, and
pungent anxiety of mind, than those whose duty it is to
fulfil it without remissness or partiality.

EXTRAORDINARY power must be entrusted somewhere,
upon extraordinary occasions; and parliament vest it most
reasonably, as they confine it to a season of necessity only,
and to those whose *responsibility forbids its abuse*.—For at
the end of its suspension, could any serious charge be
brought against the executive power for malice, wanton-
ness, or cruelty, parliament would shew as much indignation against them, as they have now shewn with regard
to the conspirators.

BUT the great and distinguished characters, that now compose the present ministry, would revolt at the idea of performing one act of severity, or injustice. The humanity
of Mr. Dundas, in his situation of secretary of state, has
been warmly avowed more than once by opposition themselves. His philanthropy and his firmness go hand in hand;

and

and his acknowledged manlinefs, his candour, and his integrity, render it utterly impoffible for him ever to violate his nature, by the commiffion of any harfh action. Let us not therefore be afraid of an adminiftration whofe fole aim is to PRESERVE THE CONSTITUTION. But let us rather dread the wolves and the foxes that infidioufly fawn upon it, in order the more fecurely to deftroy it. As the *Jacobites* formerly exclaimed againft its fufpenfion, becaufe it prevented them from overturning the Conftitution, fo do the *Jacobins* now; and for the fame reafon.

To conclude, it is our duty to obferve that the executive power has acted, on the prefent occafion, with wifdom void of rafhnefs, and with firmnefs void of rigour. The difaffected have prefumed much upon a fuppofed tamenefs in the minifter, which they perceive has turned out to be fallacious. "He dare not go to war. He dare not arm the people. "He dare not fufpend the *Habeas Corpus Act.*" Thefe ufed to be the exultations of the friends of anarchy, to embolden their abettors, and excite them on to fcatter the feeds of diforder and tumult throughout the kingdom. But fortunately for the tranquillity of Britain, all thefe fteps he has wifely and vigoroufly taken; and in adopting each of them, he has not anticipated, but OBEYED, THE WISHES OF THE GREAT BODY OF THE NATION.

THE Democracy of England, we mean the Democracy of property, he wields with the fpirit of his father. As to the democracy of an inferior nature, which it has been fo much the fafhion with CERTAIN GENTLEMEN of late meanly and flagitioufly to endeavour to wield; it can never be feperated from the other, to act againft the country; while the PEOPLE of PROPERTY difplay fuch *energy*, and THE ADMINISTRATION fuch *vigilance*, under an AMIABLE MONARCH, the VIRTUOUS and PATRIOT GUARDIAN of the RIGHTS and LIBERTIES of the Britifh Empire.

APPENDIX.

THE WAR.

The expences of the war, muft neceffarily be great; but it muft alfo be allowed, that the neceffity and juft caufe of it, as well as the advantages already obtained, are of a proportionate magnitude; and muft afford matter of confolation to every loyal and patriotic Briton; upon which he will felicitate himfelf in the confident belief, that the war will finally terminate in favour of his country.

The fuccefs of the allies, in reducing Condé, Quefnoy, and Valenciennes; the falvation of Holland, and the recovery of the Auftrian Netherlands; our deftruction of a great part of the French fleet at Toulon, and of their arfenals there; our annihilation of the French Newfoundland Fifhery; our capture of Tobago; nearly of all the French part of St. Domingo, in the Weft, and of Pondichery in the Eaft Indies; reducing their power there almoft to extinction: Thefe feveral important objects, were accomplifhed in the laft campaign; previous to which, in a few months, by a miraculous celerity, we increafed our navy from 15,000 to 69,000 men; and our line of battle fhips, from 13 to 80, with frigates in proportion. If all thefe acquifitions are duly confidered, together with the wonderful energies of the executive government, it will evidently appear, that Britain performed more in the campaign of 1793, than was ever before done in the firft year, or indeed during the two firft years of any former war!

But the various and important fucceffes of Britain, this year, are fo great, as to flatter us that the war will foon have a happy termination. The capture of Martinico and St. Lucia, in the Weft Indies; the almoft entire reduction

tion of Corsica, in the Mediterranean; not to mention the fall of Landrecy; but, above all, Earl Howe's glorious

VICTORY OVER THE FRENCH FLEET.

In concluding this, our View of the present State of Affairs, we feel ourselves exultingly happy, in having it in our power to relate one of the most brilliant actions, recorded in the annals of Naval History; and of which, on account of its importance, as well as celebrity, we shall detail somewhat at large.

On the morning of the 28th of May, Lord Howe discovered the French fleet to the windward of the British, and partial actions ensued that evening and the next day.

The weather gage having been obtained by the English, in the progress of the last-mentioned day, and their fleet being in a situation for bringing the enemy to close action on the first of June, the ships bore up together for that purpose, between seven and eight o'clock in the morning.

The French, their force consisting of 26 ships of the line, opposed to the English fleet of 25, (the Audacious having parted company with the sternmost ship of the enemy's line, captured in the night of the 28th,) waited for the action, and sustained the attack with wonderful resolution.

In less than an hour after the close action commenced in the center, the French Admiral, on board the Montagne, who engaged the Queen Charlotte, commanded by Earl Howe, crowded off, and was followed by most of the ships of his van, in condition to carry sail after him; leaving with the English, ten or twelve of his crippled or totally dismasted ships,

ships, exclusive of two sunk in the engagement. The Queen Charlotte had then lost her fore topmast, and the main topmast fell over the side very soon after.

The greater number of the other ships of the British fleet, were, at this time, so much disabled or widely separated, and under such circumstances, with respect to those ships of the enemy in a state of action, and with which the firing was still continued, that two or three, even of their dismasted ships, attempting to get away under a sprit-sail, singly, or smaller sail raised on the stump of the foremast, could not be detained.

Eight were unable to escape, two of which sunk; one of them during the action; and the other, the Vengeur, almost immediately upon being taken possession of. The following, to which we have annexed an account of the killed and wounded, were brought safe into Portsmouth, on the 13th of June.

List of FRENCH SHIPS, captured on the First Day of June, 1794.

Ships' Names.	Guns.	Killed.	Wounded.	Total.
La Juste	80	100	145	245
Sans Pareille	80	260	120	380
L'Amerique	74	134	110	244
L'Achille	74	36	30	66
Northumberland	74	60	100	160
L'Impetueux	74	100	75	175
Vengeur (sunk)	74	320	—	320
			Grand Total,	1590

Le Jacobin, sunk in action, and not a man saved.

A List of the BRITISH FLEET, with the Returns of the killed and wounded, on Board his Majesty's Ships, in the Actions with the French Fleet, on the 28th and 29th of MAY, and the 1st of JUNE, 1794.

Ships' Names.	Seamen killed.	Marines killed.	Seamen wounded	Marines wounded	Total.	Officers killed.	Officers wounded
Cæsar	18	—	37	—	55	—	—
Bellerophon	3	1	26	1	31	—	3
Leviathan	10	—	32	1	43	—	1
Royal Sovereign	11	3	39	5	58	1	3
Marlborough	24	5	76	14	119	1	9
Defence	14	4	29	10	57	2	3
Impregnable	7	—	24	—	31	1	2
Tremendous	2	1	6	2	11	1	—
Barfleur	8	1	22	3	34	—	4
Culloden	2	—	6	—	8	—	1
Invincible	9	5	21	10	45	—	—
Gibraltar	1	1	12	—	14	—	—
The Charlotte	13	1	24	5	43	2	2
Brunswick	30	—	91	—	121	3	4
Valiant	1	1	5	4	11	—	—
Queen	30	6	57	10	103	1	5
Orion	5	—	20	4	29	—	—
Ramillies	2	—	7	—	9	—	—
Alfred	—	—	6	2	8	—	—
Russel	7	1	24	2	34	—	3
Royal George	18	2	63	9	92	2	5
Montague	4	—	13	—	17	1	2
Majestic	3	—	4	1	8	—	—
Glory	13	—	31	8	52	2	—
Thunderer	—	—	—	—	—	—	—
Audacious	4	—	18	—	22	—	—
Grand Total,	207	32	596	91	926	17	47

The

The Rank and Number of Officers killed and wounded.

KILLED.

Two Captains—5 Midshipmen—4 Masters—1 Master's Mate—4 Lieutenants—1 Boatswain.

WOUNDED.

Three Admirals—6 Captains—11 Lieutenants—16 Midshipmen—2 Masters—3 Master's Mates—4 Boatswains—2 Ensigns.

Names of Captains killed.

James Montague, Esq. of the Montague.
Alexander Saunders, of the 29th Regiment.

Admirals wounded.

Thomas Graves, Esq. Admiral of the Blue.
Thomas Pasley, Esq. Rear Admiral of the White.
George Bowyer, Esq. Rear Admiral of the White.

Captains wounded.

Hon. G. Berkley, of the Marlborough.
John Hutt, Esq. of the Queen.
Sir Andrew Douglas, Second Captain of the Charlotte.
John Hervey, Esq. of the Brunswick.
Mr. Smith, of the Marines, on Board the Bellerophon.
Mr. C. Money, of the Marines, on Board the Royal Sovereign.

Considerable as the loss of the English may appear, the reader will perceive that it bears but a small proportion to that of the enemy; and would be still less so, could we obtain accurate returns of those that fell on board the ships that escaped.

A few days before the action, Lord Howe retook 18 of the Castor's convoy, a French sloop, and two corvetts; these he sunk, after taking the men out, saying he could not man them from his own fleet, as he was determined to bring on a decisive action with the enemy.

That modest simplicity, which is the true characteristic of genuine worth, and which so peculiarly distinguishes Earl Howe's official letter, could be exceeded only by his deportment, so amiably evinced as his Lordship passed from the New Sally Port, his place of landing, to the Governor's house at Portsmouth, amidst the acclamations of an immense populace; besides the military, assembled on this occasion, with their bands of music; who, among other martial airs, saluted him with that of, " See, the Conquering Hero comes!"—When his Lordship could be heard, he repeatedly thanked the people for the great respect shewn him, observing, that the Victory was due to the bravery of the British Seamen, and not to himself alone.

We cannot but mention here, to the honour of Earl Howe, that as his late action was, as important to Great Britain, as that of Lord Hawke in 1759, which we have just recorded; so was it, in many respects, more glorious.— Admiral Hawke had one sail of the line more than the French; Earl Howe had one sail less. Hawke captured one sail of the line, sunk two, and burnt two. Howe has captured seven sail of the line, one of which sunk soon after

its

its striking to the British flag; and one sunk during the action. Hawke lost two line of battle ships that were stranded, and afterwards burnt by his orders. Howe has not lost one. Therefore, in Hawke's engagement, as we lost two ships, and gained only one, the other four disabled French ships being sunk or burnt, our fleet in fact returned with one ship of the line less in number, than it sailed with from Torbay; and the French fleet with five less than it sailed with from Brest; so that the engagement in 1759, considering the loss of one English ship in number, made but four less to France, when the strength of each was ascertained after the action.

But in the late engagement of Lord Howe, the principal part of whose conquering fleet, with their prizes, arrived at Spithead, on the 13th of June, the other ships putting into Plymouth, where they are refitting with all possible expedition; we have acquired six sail of the line more, and the French return into port with eight sail less. The 25 sail of the British fleet, are now increased, by that action, to 31 sail; while that of France, consisting of 26 sail, is now reduced to 18 sail; from whence it may be fairly stated, that a superior force of the enemy is now reduced, by the skill of Lord Howe, and the valour of our brave countrymen, *nearly one third* of its former strength; while we, at the same time, have *gained one fifth* in point of number of ships, by the immortal action of the First of June, 1794. This is the true way to calculate its value, besides the great loss, by death and capture of the French seamen, in comparison to our loss in that engagement.

When the intelligence arrives at Paris, of the disaster that has happened to their grand fleet, it is not improbable, considering that the minor faction is only checked, not extinguished, but that another Revolution may soon take place; and more congenial, perhaps, to the restoration of order and

an

an equitable government; and that a dawn, towards a general treaty of peace, upon lasting security, to the independence of the neighbouring nations, will foon appear.

At any rate, the late great naval battle will fo invigorate the allies, that the propofed march towards the French capital, will probably be very much accelerated; while Britain, following her blow with fpirit, with alacrity, and with wifdom, will fcour the whole French coaft, affift the now-increafing Royalifts, and ftrike terror and difmay into the very heart of the Convention itfelf.

But in this crifis, it is ftill the duty of every loyal fubject to *take every precaution againft all* POSSIBLE INVASION, *as well as* INSURRECTION. For although the Old Monarchy, after the defeat of Conflans, laid afide the fcheme of Invafion; yet we do not know to what acts of defperation the anarchy may be driven, when they hear of the lofs of their fleet; as they are a band of monfters, who, caring no more for the lofs of an 100,000 lives, than for as many animals, would facrifice that or any number, in a vain attempt to make a defcent here; that, by fuch a fcheme, they might divert the public mind from lifting its avenging arm, in the day of defpair, and letting it fall on the heads of their brutal tyrants.

Still, therefore, *let us neither relax in our* ARMING, *nor in the* DISCIPLINING *of our fellow fubjects*. By thefe means only, we can almoft bid defiance to all the viciffitudes of a juft and neceffary war, on the happy event of which our Liberty, our Property, and every thing elfe that can be dear to free men, folely depends. Let us continue increafing our armaments, and, with our native courage, and our infular fituation, we need not fear of continuing to be free.

APPENDIX.

APPENDIX.

AS an INVASION of BRITAIN has been the darling object of France, since the reign of Lewis XIV. and as their object is the same, during the NEW ANARCHY, as under the OLD MONARCHY, it may be considered as very proper and useful, by way of APPENDIX to this HISTORY OF INVASIONS, to shew how their attempts may be defeated, *were even* A LANDING *to take place;* and to give the opinions of the most celebrated commanders, who have written upon tactics, as to some of the most prominent branches of military duty and discipline, that can be connected with a DEFENSIVE ARMY, *cavalry* as well as *infantry*, in case of invasion.

It must be observed, that, at the present moment, when such invasion has been so long threatened, by the Demagogues of France, an *entire confidence in* GOVERNMENT *is absolutely necessary to our* PRESERVATION; and the *common danger* should produce an UNION OF ALL, in the *defence* of their KING, their CONSTITUTION, and their COUNTRY.

Some, from sordid motives; others, from motives *inimical to our Constitution*, have treated all reports of invasion as chimerical. To the latter, it is needless to reply, as they treacherously wish to put their country off its guard, by instilling such ideas. To the former, it can only be said, that allowing no invasion to happen, which is the hope of every loyal and peaceable subject; yet, surely it is wise and provident, to prepare against the worst, by being *armed and disciplined*, in order to be ready to repel any attempt that may be made, by a marauding horde, on our *Property* and our *Liberty*. As in crossing Blackheath, at night, when highwaymen have been heard to threaten that road, it is prudent to go armed; so when the piratical ruffians of France, menace the plunder of our country, and the butchery of its inhabitants, it is indispensibly necessary to be prepared for their reception.

At this crisis, then, every real friend to his country, should strengthen the hand of Government, by *subscribing to its defence;* and by adopting every possible mode to

a render

render us AN ARMED NATION, not to commit outrages upon society, but to PRESERVE OUR OWN FREEDOM. *The man who sneers at the danger, and decries ARMING, is the man who wishes to see us undone; that he may vainly hope, by anarchy, to rise upon the ruin of his country.*

IN treating how all attempts to invade us, may be rendered abortive, it is absolutely necessary to inculcate VIGILANCE, in counteracting the *treacherous* and *disaffected;* and here we cannot help *applauding* GOVERNMENT, for their late WISE and VIGOROUS MEASURES. For, in the events of an invasion, or even at present, on the prospect of one, evil disposed persons will use all their art to seduce, to mislead, and to poison the public mind; so that should it actually happen, they may the more easily divide the country, in order to palsy its exertions; to betray intelligence; to create mutiny; to promote desertion; to aid the foe with necessaries; or openly to join them.

BESIDES vigilance, the lower classes ought to be instructed in their duty, on such an occasion; that they may be guarded against the snares of all incendiaries. *For the* POOR MAN *has his* PROPERTY *at stake, as well as the* RICH. *His* MANUAL LABOUR *is his* PROPERTY. And if, in case of anarchy, as in France, he receive no fair and adequate reward for involuntary fatigue, and unavailing industry; if he be compelled to labour for the ruin, instead of the benefit of his fellow creatures; if he be dragged forth at all hours, to commit the crimes of robbery and murder; and if he cannot enjoy either personal security, or the comfortable recompence arising from honest industry; he is as much deprived of his property and freedom, as if he were the richest man in the kingdom. This is strictly the case of the lower classes in France.

NEXT to vigilance and instruction, which promote, in a great degree, *unanimity, religion, loyalty, zeal, discipline, subordination,* and *firmness,* are to be recommended.

THE LANDHOLDER, the MANUFACTURER, THE ARTIZAN, and the FARMER, being in a manner, the *protectors* and the *instructors* of the *lower orders,* they ought to embrace every opportunity of instilling these into the minds of their dependants; and by thus cherishing the flame of true patriotism, the nation can meet any invasion with the utmost confidence and security.

BUT above all, it is the business of THE CLERGY, incessantly, during the present conflict, to blend the *patriot duties* with the *religious* and the *moral obligations,* in all their discourses. In the last century, they *did too much.* In the present century, they *do too little.*

IT

It is not meant here, in treating of our best modes of defence, and discipline, to dwell on the superiority of our navy, *and the impossibility of our receiving any great blow by land, while we are so powerful at sea.* But allowing, which is highly improbable, that the French were to endeavour the making good a landing, or had made one with a great force, we shall select from some of the best writers, their opinions, as to the mode to be adopted for our security, in either of these cases.

EDMONDS.

The classical Mr. Edmonds, Remembrancer of the city of London, who wrote in the reign of Queen Elizabeth, and who was very curious in ancient tactics, as well as the tactics in use at that period, has left a very scarce and ingenious treatise on the question, *Whether or not it were best to oppose an enemy on his attempting to land upon the coast, with an intention of invading and conquering the country.* It was written soon after the defeat of the *Armada*; when the nation, from that recent attempt, must have been well versed in the general topic of defence from invasion; and which was then again menaced by Philip of Spain. Mr. *Edmonds'* words are:

Upon the circumstance of *landing*, I shall handle that controversy which has been often debated by our English commanders, "whether it be better, in question of an inva-
"sion, and in the absence of our shipping, to oppose an
"enemy at his landing on our coast, or quietly suffer him
"to put his men ashore, and retire with our forces to some
"inland place, and there wait to give him battle?"

Such as first started this question, and were of opinion that we ought not by any means to encounter an enemy at landing, as we might much endanger ourselves and country, did not consider the difference between countries that border upon each other on the same continent, and those that are disjoined by so great a bar as the ocean.

FIRST.

It may be objected, that it is very difficult to resist an enemy at his landing, from the uncertainty of place as well as of time. Being ignorant where he will attempt to land, we muſt equally defend all acceſſible places; to effect which, it is requiſite that, according to the particular quality of every ſpot liable to be invaded, our defenſive forces muſt every where be ſufficient in ſtrength to repel the enemy. Conſidering, therefore, the great extenſion of our maritime parts, and the many landing places on our coaſt, it will require a much greater number of men to defend them than this country can afford.

ANSWER.

It cannot indeed be denied but the place of the enemy's landing will be doubtful, and therefore our great care muſt extend itſelf generally, to all acceſſible places. But that our defenſive forces are not ſufficient to guard in a competent manner all ſuch places as the danger may require, ſhall be proved fallacious.

OUR FORCES ARE SUFFICIENT, WITH GOOD GENERALSHIP AND POSITION, TO DEFEND ALL PARTS OF THE ISLAND.

To prove that our forces are ſufficient, we muſt neceſſarily enter into particulars. Being very well acquainted with the coaſt of Kent, I ſhall lay down a plan for its defence, which may be exactly followed by all maritime counties where an invaſion can be expected.

It is a ſhore of nearly as large extent as any other county within the kingdom. From the point of Neſſe, by Lyd, which is the uttermoſt ſkirt upon the coaſt of Suſſex, to Margate, upon the coaſt of Eſſex, is, by computation, about twenty-four miles. But in this great extent of coaſt, not above one *ſixth* part of it is calculated for the landing of ſuch a force, as would be neceſſary to invade this country, with any proſpect of ſucceſs; partly owing to the hugeneſs of the cliffs, which incloſe a great part of that ſkirt; and partly, as much of that ground which may be landed upon, has ſuch imminent and difficult places near adjoining, that any army which might endeavour to land there, would find itſelf ſo ſtreightened, being oppoſed but

with

with a small force, that it could not easily extricate itself, so as to advance into firm and tenable fighting ground, without apparent ruin of the whole invading army.

BESIDES, it cannot be denied, but that generally, along the coast of *Kent*, there are so many rocks, shelves, flats, and other impediments, that a navy of large ships can have no anchorage near the shore. The coast likewise lies so open to the weather, that the least gale of wind may drive them from their anchors. All this duly considered, it appears that this large coast will afford a far lesser part fit for the landing of an army, than was at first imagined. Were it necessary, I could make it evident, by a particular description of the number, quantity, and quality of the places on the coast; and thereby put the matter beyond all dispute.

MEANS TO GUARD EVERY MARITIME COUNTY IN THE SAME MANNER AS KENT, WHERE THERE IS THE LEAST DANGER OF AN INVASION.

To shew that our forces, by a proper disposition, are able to afford every maritime county a safe and sure guard from invasion, I shall give a general plan of that means, adapted to the county of Kent; but which will serve as a guide, in a great degree, to the defence of other counties upon the coast, where the enemy is most likely to land.

I would observe this order: to make a *triple* division of all the force appointed for this county. I shall suppose, for example, the number designed for the defence of Kent, to be 12,000. Of these, I should station 3000 about the point of *Nesse*; 3000 about *Margate*; and 6000 about the center of the county, which I conceive to be *Folkstone*. My greatest care should be, so to dispose of them, as they might not only aid one another in the same county; but, as every county borders upon another, so in case of emergency, they should mutually help one another.

IF the enemy, for instance, should attempt a landing about *Nesse*, not only the 6000 stationed about *Folkstone* should

should march to the aid of the 3000 stationed about that place; but, it being the nearest part of Kent to the county of SUSSEX, such forces too, as were in the neighbourhood, in that county, and so likewise of the rest. From this we may perceive how great a force would be assembled in a few hours, for the reinforcement of any place that might be invaded. As to the quartering of the troops, especial care must be had to the places of danger, according to their importance. My meaning is not to lodge them close together, but to stretch them along the coast, by regiments and companies, as the country could best afford to entertain them.

As to the uncertainty of the time when the invaders may attempt a landing, in answer to the latter part of the first objection, I hold it absolutely requisite that our forces should be disciplined, assembled, and stationed properly, before the enemy should be discovered near our coast, ready to make a landing. For, at such a moment, it would be a gross absurdity to imagine that men could be suddenly assembled without confusion, and make so long a march with such expedition as the necessity of the occasion would require.

SECONDLY.

It may be objected that all our landing-places are of such disadvantage for the defensive troops, that it would be of no avail to endeavour the repulse of an invading army at its landing. Such places being open and plain, they yield no shelter from the fury of the enemy's artillery, with which their long-boats and landing vessels will be plentifully supplied; and, beating upon the beach, as most of the landing-places are open and plain, the invaders would so annoy us, that our troops would not, unsheltered, be able to sustain their fire.

ANSWER.

As to the disadvantage of the place, in regard to the artillery of the invaders, it is true that such places as would afford the enemy an easy shore to land on, are chiefly plain, open, and deprived of all covert. What then? Shall a soldier use no art to counteract the disadvantages of nature? I make no doubt but an ingenious commander would use such skill and industry upon the most indefensible place, the beach itself, as might give sufficient security to his forces, and outweigh the advantages that the enemy might otherwise possess; besides we can easily overcome all these difficulties, and use the benefit of the firm land to repel an enemy, weakened with the sea, tossed with the billows, troubled with his weapons,

pons, besides many other discouragements that are presented to him, both from the land and the sea.

THIRDLY.

An objection may arise from the disparity of numbers, and condition of the forces of either party. For it must be granted, that the defendants being obliged to guard so many places at once, cannot furnish such numbers to every particular place for defence, as the offensive invaders. As to the quality of the forces, it is without dispute that a great and potent Prince, for such a one it must be, that undertaketh to invade the territories of so absolute (these are his words) and well-obeyed a Princess as her Majesty, (Queen Elizabeth) is; he would embark the flower of his soldiery, besides be assisted with the gallant troops of volunteers, which commonly attend such service. How then can it be imagined, the time and place of their attempt being uncertain, that the defendants should equal such invaders, in spirit, skill, and experience?

ANSWER.

As to the third objection, this briefly shall be sufficient; that we are not so much to regard that our forces equal them in number, as to see that they are sufficient for the nature of the place, in case of an enemy's landing. For in places of difficult access, we know that a small number is able to oppose a great force: and we doubt not but, all circumstances duly considered, we shall proportionably equal the enemy both in the number and the quality of their forces; always, however, presupposing, that the state shall never be destitute of a sufficient number of troops, trained and exercised in a competent manner, to defend their country from foreign enemies.

Thus much concerning the answers to those three reasons, which seem to prove that an enemy is not to be resisted at his landing. If we but look a little to the hazards and inconveniences that attends him at that juncture, and the advantages he gains by a firm and proper landing, we shall easily discover the folly of this opinion.

First, By allowing him to land unmolested, we give him leave to live upon the spoil of the country, which, in so plentiful a kingdom as England, cannot be prevented by any wasting, spoiling, or withdrawing, of our provisions; as we have no strong towns at all, sufficient to secure them.

Secondly, Obedience, which at other times, is willingly given to Princes, is then often greatly weakened; and all necessary means to maintain a war, is sometimes in an invasion, rather unwillingly drawn from the subject.

Thirdly,

Thirdly, Opportunity is given to malecontents, either to make head themselves, or to fly over to the enemy.

Fourthly, It would be madness to hazard a kingdom upon one stroke, after suffering the enemy to land, having it in our power to prevent him; besides not considering many other disadvantages which such an occasion would discover to us, when it was too late.

LLOYD.

General Lloyd, so celebrated for pointing out all that could be done, by an invasion of England; and all that might be done, by defending it against invaders, was an officer in the Prussian service, in 1754. A plan being then forming, by France, for invading this country, Mr. Lloyd was sent out here, by the Duc de Bellisle, then minister at war, to examine all the coast and the contiguous country, opposite France, which he effectually accomplished in the year 1756; and once before, in the year 1745. He afterwards died, in the service of England, and a pensioner upon the Chelsea establishment.

The following opinions of General Lloyd, upon the defence of England, against invasion from France, must, therefore, be very acceptable at this moment. This treatise was written about the year 1779, when the combined French and Spanish fleets were in the Channel, and when we were in some dread of an invasion.

HIS INTRODUCTION.

WHILE the terrors of an invasion and its consequences, hang over our heads, it is the duty of every man to contribute, with his person and advice, to the support of the state; and point out the means which appear proper, to defeat the designs of our enemies. With this view I have written the following discourse on the supposed invasion, and hope it may serve, in some measure, to render it fruitless;

less; and inspire government, as well as the nation in general, with that confidence which the situation of our affairs require.

As an invasion of England, with a powerful army, may be attended with fatal consequences, I shall confine my observations to that alone, and endeavour to shew how it may be frustrated.

DIFFICULTIES THAT AN INVADING ARMY MUST ENCOUNTER, IN ENGLAND, FROM ITS BEING A CLOSE COUNTRY, AND FULL OF DEFILES, OR NARROW PASSES.

ENGLAND, in general, is not only very hilly, but also, for the most part, full of inclosures. As you come from Exeter, for instance, towards London, it is so inclosed with hedges and ditches, that for many miles together, you do not find ground sufficiently open to form twenty battalions upon; so that the high road, where an enemy can alone march, is one continued pass, or defile, winding at the foot of the mountains, or through the inclosures. Those mountains and hedges being properly occupied, an enemy cannot advance a step; and if he is once engaged in them, he can never extricate himself out of the narrow labyrinth, and will be forced to lay down his arms.

We therefore possess so many advantages over an invading foe, that if we avail ourselves of them, there can be no room left to fear the event of the invasion, with which we are now threatened.

1st. The face of the country is generally *close*, where an army, in the course of many miles, cannot find room to form and act in; or so full of *defiles*, or narrow passes, formed by mountains, hills, forests, rivers, morasses, hedges, &c. where the road is so contracted that few men only can advance in front.

2ndly. It forces them, therefore, to march in one column; and this difficulty alone overbalances almost every other advantage.

3dly. The

3dly. The invading French can bring but little cavalry; which, from the nature of the country, may not, if we chuse it, ever have an opportunity of acting.

4thly. They can have no artillery, and not many field-pieces, compared to what we can bring into the field.

5thly. They can have no other provisions but what they bring with them; which, however abundant it may seem, will last only for a short time.

6thly. They can never have a sufficient number of horses and carriages to transport their stores, artillery, baggage, provisions, &c. which will retard their march, so that they cannot advance above a mile or two in the day.

7thly. When they proceed from the shore, they can form no magazines in the country, and must be supplied from their original *depôt*; and when their line of communication is protracted, to a certain length, half their army will not be sufficient to escort their convoys, which you may, and must intercept. This will not only retard their progress, but very soon stop them entirely, and force their army to go back. They have but this alternative; to gain a great and decisive victory, or abandon the enterprize. They cannot remain on the spot, in a close country, surrounded by mountains on every side, and those occupied by our troops; and we have nothing to do, but to profit of these advantages, and avoid a general action.

8thly. They cannot send detachments, or deviate from the great road, or pass, without being exposed to certain destruction; whereas we, availing ourselves of every cross road and path, can, without risk, attack their whole line of march, and soon throw it into confusion. They can act on that only; whereas, we can act when and where we please.

9thly. Though the frontier of England is very extensive, and therefore, seems very difficult to be defended; yet, upon a due examination, it will be always found, that such a frontier can be attacked only in a few points, and that these points are fixed and determined by the nature and position or the countries at war. An army, like a traveller, must necessarily depart from a given point, and proceed to a given point in the enemy's country. The line which unites these points, I call the line of operation. It is manifest, that all deviation from this, and all delays in pursuing the march, are so much time lost; and in the end, will force an enemy to return, either for want of subsistence, or by bad weather, &c. To diminish the difficulties which oppose the progress of the main army on

the

the line of operation, sometimes a corps is made to act on another line, to create a line of diversion; but such a corps can never produce a solid advantage, if you attend to the main point, and frustrate the designs of the principal army.

10thly. An offensive war, it appears from hence, must be prosecuted with the utmost vigour and activity, on the part of the invading army; and nothing less than complete victories can render it successful.

11thly. A defensive war must consequently be carried on with caution and prudence; and, above all things, a general action is to be avoided. You oppose the enemy in front, by occupying strong posts, and with the remainder of your forces you act on his flanks and rear; which, in a short time, will reduce him, though much stronger, to fall back, and approach his *dépôts*. If King Harold had followed this doctrine, it is probable we should have known William the Conqueror by his defeat only.

12thly. An invading army, which acts over a branch of the sea, must occupy some convenient and safe harbour. He must gain a great and decisive battle; or by skilful manœuvres, force the enemy to abandon such a tract of country as will, in a great measure, support the assailant. For if he depends in the smallest degree on shipping, and a precarious navigation for supplies, he cannot prosecute any solid operation; and successive campaigns will be consumed in fruitless and unmeaning excursions. Troops must, however, return to the shore, to take up their winter quarters; and at last, his men and money being exhausted, he perishes totally, or abandons the enterprize with loss and ignominy.

BREST.

Let us now apply the principles established above, to the present case.

It is evident, that Brest is the point from whence the French must depart; because all their operations, even when they have landed, are connected with, and depend upon their fleet. But as all operations, which depend on navigation,

navigation, are from its nature precarious, and liable to a thousand difficulties, they must have likewise a place of arms in this country, a spacious harbour as near their own coast as possible, &c. and besides these advantages, absolutely required, the place must be so situated, that by marching a few miles inland, they can occupy such a post as will render them masters of a tract of country behind their army, sufficient to supply it with subsistence, on their stops; without which, no progress can be made, nor can they remain for any considerable time in any part of the country. The plan which offers these advantages, is the most eligible they can fix upon.

PLYMOUTH.

Answers perfectly this description. It is a safe and convenient harbour, near the coast of France; and could they possess it, by marching only to Chudleigh, the invaders would be masters of Cornwall, Devonshire, and part of Somersetshire, where they can find provisions in abundance; which will enable them to prosecute their operations, and penetrate further into the country; or if they chose to remain there, it would be a difficult matter to drive them back, as they would have a fleet at Plymouth.

PORTSMOUTH.

The only place next to Plymouth, which can serve the purpose of the enemy, is Portsmouth. It has two fine roads, St. Helen's and Spithead, and a very safe harbour. The town and the dock, on the land-side, are fortified, and cannot be taken without a regular siege: the undertaking of which is very difficult, though we had no ships to defend it.

The

The island of Portsea, lies very low, and does not furnish the necessary materials to carry on the works, required on such occasions. The enemy must occupy Gosport, with part of his army, while the remainder carries on the siege; and if we are masters of Portsdown, and can confine him to the island, we are always able to succour the place, and force him to retire, which he would find very difficult.

[*N. B. Since General Lloyd wrote the above, Government have made it their great object to fortify Portsmouth and Plymouth in such a manner, as to render those great arsenals almost impregnable against any force whatever.*]

ISLE OF WIGHT.

When I considered, at first, the position of the Isle of Wight, I thought that an enemy might occupy it, and with 15,000 or 20,000 men, keep possession of the whole ground; but having lately examined it, with proper attention, I believe now that it is absolutely impossible. This island runs from east to west, and is generally intersected with very high mountains, whose basis run quite to the shore. On the south side of the island, they rise by ranges, like an amphitheatre, almost perpendicular, forty or fifty feet high; and the summits, excepting in a very few places, to above a thousand; so that if any troops are posted on them, there is no possibility of landing.

The only place where it is less difficult, is in Brading Bay, opposite St. Helen's Road. This is a small creek, between two very high hills, which being occupied, will prevent a landing. On the south side is a bay, where the shore is low, and very proper for debarking troops; but Sand-down Fort defends that bay very well. From thence to the westernmost point, and the Needles, no place can be found where a landing can be attempted, if there is the least opposition: Besides the coast is so open and dangerous, that a boat, much less a fleet, cannot lay at anchor, an hour, without the utmost risk of perishing.

From the Needles to Ride, you may land any where, and a fleet may anchor in safety, there being a sufficient

depth

depth of water to come through the Needles, all the way to Spithead. The channel between the Needles and Hurst Castle, is narrow, but it is safe for the largest vessels; but in case of an enemy attempting that passage, it would be next to an impossibility to succeed.

Though the difficulties which occur in landing on the south side of the Isle of Wight, and indeed of approaching it, yet if no opposition is made, it might be effected; however, if we consider the extent of the island, the great number of very high mountains, and of places to land from our side, it will appear that 20,000 men would not be able to occupy it in such a manner as to prevent our taking it from them. They must fortify all the shore opposite the New Forest, as well as all the downs or mountains behind them; for there is no spot on the whole island where the most extensive fortress could in any degree, secure the possession of it to the French. If it is placed on the south shore, there is neither bay nor harbour; and by our occupying some neighbouring mountains, the garrison would be starved in it.

The same difficulty will occur if placed in the center, or on the Northern shore, at Cowes, Yarmouth, &c. from whence I conclude, that while England exists as a nation, *an enemy cannot keep the Isle of Wight a month, though there were 30,000 men in it.*

HARWICH.

From Portsmouth to Harwich, there is no harbour or road which can, in any degree, answer the purposes of an enemy, who intends to land a considerable army, and make war in the country. The difficulty, though very great, does not consist in debarking 40,000 men. It is also necessary *that they should have a* COMMODIOUS *and* SAFE HARBOUR; *a* PLACE *of* ARMS; *and be so situated, as to keep a* SURE *and* EASY COMMUNICATION *with* FRANCE, *especially with* BREST.

Such a place is *not* to be found on *the whole coast, except Plymouth and Portsmouth,* of which enough has been already said. The Dutch fleet came up the river very well; *but how long did they remain there? a few hours only;* consider, besides, the great difference there is between coming from the coast

coast of Holland, with twenty men of war, to make a ridiculous bravado, which lasted 24 hours, or coming from Brest with a fleet, and four or five hundred transports to invade us, and carry on a war in the heart of our country. The one is easy, the *other impracticable*.

[*N. B. This opinion of so great an engineer as General Lloyd, that an attempt to invade us with a great force by the* RIVER THAMES IS IMPRACTICABLE, *although it ought to quiet the minds of the inhabitants in the metropolis, as to no immediate danger, yet they ought not to be the less alert in* ARMING *and* SUBSCRIBING *for the* GENERAL DEFENCE *of the country. For, were the French marauders to make good a landing, through the remissness of our fellow-subjects, the* PLUNDERING OF THE CAPITAL *would be the chief object of their ambition.*]

A GREAT INVASION CAN ONLY BE IN THE WEST.

THOUGH I am convinced that AN INVASION *neither will nor can be made* in *Sussex, Kent*, or *higher up*; I do not think it impossible, that, in order *to facilitate the operations of their* MAIN ARMY, the enemy may *threaten* DIFFERENT *and* DISTANT PARTS *of the* COAST;—*but no* SOLID OPERATION *can, in my opinion, be* EXECUTED *but in* THE WEST.

GENERAL DEFENCE, UPON THAT SUPPOSITION.

WHENEVER a tract of country is to be defended, reason points out the necessity of occupying some *central* positions, with *strong corps* to the *right* and *left*, to *stop* the enemy till the *whole* can be collected. The line we have to defend, extends from *Plymouth* to *Dover*. *Portsdown* is the *central* point in that line. I would therefore recommend that a *third* part of our army be placed there, and in the *New Forest*.

Another

Another *third*, on *Hall Down Hill*, beyond *Exeter*. And the remaining *third*, in the limits between *Suffex* and *Kent*, on that branch of the river Medway, called *the Teife*.

If an attempt is made to the *Weftward*, the body encamped at *Portfmouth* will march thither, and join that on *Hall Down*, which I fuppofe inftantly in motion, where the invafion is attempted. The body placed in *Suffex* may remain there; and, by a movement to the right or to the left, be any where, as occafion may require; and eafily repulfe every attempt made on that coaft.

[N. B. *This idea of dividing the defenfive army into three parts, is nearly the fame with that of Mr. Edmonds, whom we have already quoted.*]

SUPPOSING A LANDING AT PLYMOUTH OR PORTSEA.

Should the enemy land at Plymouth, which I think moft probable that he would attempt, the force there would be able to difpute the ground till the troops on Hall Down can come to their affiftance; and it does not require 24 hours march. Oppofed in *front* by the corps at *Plymouth*, which is covered by the *works* raifing there,* as well as by the natural ftrength of the country, and attacked in the *rear* by the troops coming from *Hall Down*; an enemy, though far fuperior in number, would find himfelf greatly embarraffed.

Surrounded by the fea, by ftrong forts, and a ftronger country, occupied by 15,000 or 20,000 men, without ground sufficiently to form a line, *I do not conceive it poffible how he could avoid a total overthrow*. There is not a fpot about Plymouth, if properly occupied, and protected by the moft inconfiderable works, but will require *a fiege* to force you, which cannot be undertaken while you have any body of troops in the neighbourhood.

---

* Thefe are now completed.

PORTSEA.

PORTSEA.

The same difficulties, and much greater, will occur to an enemy in the island of *Portsea*. He can neither subsist there, nor from the adjacent country, if we have a camp on Portsdown, and another in the New Forest.

From what we have said, it seems evident that no invasion can take place, until our fleet, entirely drove out of the sea, is forced to hide itself for a considerable time in some harbour; and *that such an invasion cannot be prosecuted with any probability of success, unless the enemy is master of* PLYMOUTH *or* PORTSMOUTH.

THE ENEMY IN POSSESSION OF PLYMOUTH.

But let us suppose the enemy in full possession of Plymouth. He cannot remain there for ever. In a short time, he will be forced to penetrate further into the country, in order to procure supplies of provisions, or abandon his post, for want of them.

Forty or fifty thousand men are *not* sufficient to remain there with any safety. They must therefore advance into the country, or abandon it.

The only decisive operation they could execute, would be, to leave 10,000 men at Plymouth, and with the remainder, proceed directly to Hall Down, between Chudleigh and Exeter, which is about 36 miles from Plymouth. There is no passing between the enemy's right, and the sea; and, by an easy movement on the left, he is in the mountains, *through which all the western roads must pass towards Cornwall*. By taking this position, the enemy would be master of *Devonshire* and *Cornwall*, which would furnish subsistance in abundance, and, having *Teignmouth*, *Torbay*, and *Dartmouth* very near, he would also receive from France whatever he wanted.

Possessed

Possessed of these advantages, and having a very strong country, easily to be defended, it would become difficult to drive him back. It is therefore incumbent upon us, to post ourselves so, that we may be near enough to prevent an invading army from penetrating into the country, supposing we should not be able to hinder it from taking Plymouth, which is the height of improbability. But allowing this, as it is all a *close* country, or full of *defiles*, NUMBER *is nothing, and* DISPOSITION *every thing*. In such a country, *points* only can be attacked, and by a *given number* of men only. So that *if you occupy these points*, though otherwise *much inferior* to the enemy, you may *bring more men into action* than he, and consequently prevail. Besides, these points may be such as to enable you to attack him in *front*, *flank*, and *rear*, at the same time.

[Here General Lloyd exemplifies very minutely, the *insurmountable difficulties*, that an invading army would have to encounter, from Plymouth to Salisbury. We shall give, in his own words, his remarks on the roads from thence to London.]

From Salisbury, two roads go towards London. The *first* by Andover, Basingstoke, Bagshot, Egham, Staines, &c. Near the seven mile stone, a branch goes by Stockbridge, over some very high hills, and joins it at Basingstoke. This branch passes through an open country, which however, being *very high*, *offers many excellent camps*. The first is also carried for some miles, through an open country; but about Andover, and from thence to Basingstoke, and Hartford Bridge, it is very *close*. The other road goes by Rumsey, Farnham, &c. through a country which is still *more close* than the former; and in proportion, *affords greater advantages in attacking the enemy*.

It is needless to prosecute this description any further; *because I am persuaded that* NO ARMY, HOWEVER NUMEROUS, *will ever be able to penetrate* FORTY MILES *into the country,* IF PROPER METHODS ARE TAKEN TO OPPOSE IT; *and if we know how to avail ourselves of the* NUMBERLESS RESOURCES *which may be drawn from the* FACE OF THE COUNTRY.

I have besides, no doubt, from the known experience, firmness, and abilities of the commander in chief, Lord Amherst, that the event, should an invasion take place, will justify the high trust that his majesty has placed in him, and fully answer the expectations OF THE PUBLIC.

DIFFICULTIES OF A FRENCH ARMY IN ADVANCING FROM EXETER TO LONDON.

When we penetrate, with great and heavy armies, into an enemy's country, it is with a view to conquer some provinces, fortresses, &c. and finding nothing on the road to subsist upon, we have *fixed* and *determined* points *to lodge our stores and provisions*. Hence they are transported to the army, which must proceed from these given points, to other fixed and determined points in the enemy's country, if you carry on an offensive war. The line which unites these points, is called the line of operation. On the good or bad choice of this line, the final event of the war chiefly depends.

Let us illustrate this, by an example; an invasion of England, from the side of Plymouth. We will suppose an enemy's army to consist of 40,000 foot, and 10,000 horse, besides those required for the train of artillery, bread waggons, officers horses, &c. which will amount to as many more. This army is at Exeter, and purposes to advance to London, and has all its magazines at Exeter. I have only 30,000 men. I encamp as near Exeter as I can; and by occupying advantageous posts, which the country every where affords to a defensive army, I will force him to employ a *fortnight* in marching to Dorchester or Blandford.

I oppose, till then, the enemy in front, with small parties only on his flanks; but when he is arrived thirty or forty miles from Exeter, from which place alone he draws his subsistence; instead of opposing him in front, with all my forces, I place 10,000 men on his line of march, ten on his left flank, and the remaining ten along his line of operation, which goes from his camp to his depôts at Exeter.

The last will be distributed in four or five corps, along that line, and form a chain from one end to the other; so that a single waggon cannot pass unobserved, and consequently will be taken or attacked by some one or other of these parties.

An hundred men will destroy as many waggons, by dispersing the drivers, taking away or killing the horses, breaking the carriages, &c. The enemy must therefore send a strong body of troops, 10,000 men, for example, to escort a great convoy.

I THEN make a motion to the right, with my whole army; so that my left comes across his left, my center and right go many miles beyond it. In whatever manner the escort is distributed, as part in the front, part in the center, and part in the rear of the convoy, I say that neither ten nor even 20,000 men can preserve it; because these are chained to their convoy, and cannot quit it, nor the station they occupy. Whereas, my troops can engage, and attack, how, when, and where they please.

THEY can attack and amuse the escorts, in a pass or a wood, which of course obliges the whole to stop; while two or three thousand men, in small parties, attack the chain of waggons, from one end to the other. If they succeed in some places only, the whole will soon be dispersed.

[The general thus shews, in a masterly manner, how any invading army may be harrassed, procrastinated, or cut off in its march; and *his observations are equally applicable to one place as another.* The defensive army having all their stores brought to them by the country; the offensive army being always obliged to weaken their main body, in order to escort provisions.]

ON THE INVASION OF THE METROPOLIS.

ON the coast of England there are three harbours, where a great fleet may ride with safety. The enemy must take one of them. Suppose it done, and that the English have not a ship left. Suppose farther, that there is a French army of 60,000 men, encamped on Blackheath, and off London Bridge.

I SAY there are 200,000 men in England, *who have bore arms.* I will put the half on horseback, and the other half remains on foot; mix them as circumstances require.

Then

Then I place 50,000 men in Surrey and Suffex, and as many in Effex, who act on the enemy's line; which, on that fuppofition, muft go towards the Downes; *there being no other place where his fleet can anchor.*

Such a difpofition being made, and only half the number of men we propofe employed, I afk any officer, any man of fenfe, what will become of the enemy's army on Blackheath, or in any other given point, fixty or feventy miles from the coaft? It muft perifh; for undoubtedly no army can fubfift on a line of fuch length, as is that from France to Blackheath, over a branch of the fea; and penetrate into the country, while we have an army of 30,000 or 40,000 men only to oppofe their fupplies.

No army can fubfift in a country, unlefs it draws all, or the greateft part of its fubfiftence, from the country itfelf, and of courfe poffeffes a great tract behind it, and on every fide, to the right and left. For if you act on the enemy's line, he muft retire; and though he fhould be in poffeffion of fuch a tract of country as we fuppofe, he cannot keep it, unlefs he is mafter of one or more ftrong places, to enable him to feperate his troops, and put them into winter quarters.

LORD BOLINGBROKE.

Although Lord Bolingbroke was a politician, and not a military man; yet, as he was confeffed to be a nobleman of great genius, and is much admired for many parts of his writings, we cannot refift giving the following extract from the Craftfman, on invafion, as it was written by his lordfhip.

Nobody can be ignorant, that the neceffary preparations for an effectual invafion of this ifland, take up a great deal of time, and require fuch a number of fhips, both for tranfports and convoys, that all Europe muft be faft afleep, if it fhould pafs unobferved.

But

But let us suppose that a foreign power should conjure up a great naval armament all on a sudden, without any body's notice, and find means to steal into England, by the assistance of a dark night, or a favourable wind; yet I should be glad to know, what they are to do when they get here; for, though they might land upon us in such a clandestine manner, I presume it would not be altogether so easy for them to sculk back again; or a very difficult matter for us, to intercept their supplies.

Suppose then, that 20,000 men, of which very few can be horse, are landed in England, without any human probability of being supplied from abroad, this army can never march 20 miles into the country; for they cannot put themthemselves in a marching posture, in less than a fortnight or three weeks; and by that time, we may have 100,000 militia, drawn down upon them; whereof 10,000 shall be horse, and as many dragoons as we please; and if this militia does nothing else but drive the country; cut off their foragers and stragglers; possess themselves of the defiles; and intercept provisions; their army must be destroyed in a short time.

If this reasoning is just, in any degree, and it was never yet answered, what danger can we possibly apprehend from such an invasion; when our militia is backed with a body of several thousand regular troops, besides a sufficient number to man our garrisons, and secure Scotland?

This was the opinion of the great Duke of Marlborough, who declared, upon a very important occasion, that he would undertake to defeat any body of men, which could possibly be landed upon us by surprize, with only his own regiment of guards, two or three regiments of dragoons, and such a train of artillery as he could easily draw out against them; whereas, they could not possibly bring any with them, of any consequence. Besides, it ought to be considered, that having no fortified towns to secure themselves, *till people could come in to join them*, it would be impossible for them to stand long against such a force.

MILITARY HORSEMANSHIP,

CHIEFLY EXTRACTED FROM THE EARL OF PEMBROKE'S CELEBRATED TREATISE ON EQUITATION.

Our illustrious Author has long been held in the highest estimation; and we presume the following Extracts will be found not only of service to the FENCIBLE CAVALRY, now raising in different parts of the Kingdom, but of considerable utility to Horsemen in General.

IN THE COURSE OF THIS WORK, THE EARL OBSERVES;

IT would fcarce be poffible, neither is it indeed neceffary, to teach the more refined and difficult parts of horfemanfhip to all the different kinds, and difpofitions, both of men and horfes, which are in all regiments; or to find the time and attention requifite for it to fuch numbers; but I yet hope fome proper inftitutions will be formed, to make good riding-mafters, farriers, fadlers, and gun-fmiths, and every thing elfe neceffary for the army, upon a good, and proper footing; they are abfolutely neceffary, and fhould be properly and equally divided through the regiment, in the fquadrons and troops. There fhould be one riding-mafter in chief, with a fufficient number of under ones under him, and formed by him: he fhould infpect the work of the others very frequently, and give leffons by turns to the whole regiment, going about from one quarter to another, if the regiment is feparated: he fhould break too the officers horfes, or rather teach them to do it themfelves, who, I am forry to fay it, ftand at prefent, in general, in the greateft need of inftructions.

I muft urge the neceffity of forming, by reading, and ferious ftudy, as well as by much conftant practice, proper riding-mafters for the army.

I KNOW

I know full well that they suppose that practice alone can insure perfection; and that in their arguments in favour of this their deplorable system, they reject with scorn all books, and authors: but Equitation is confessedly a science; every science is founded upon principles, and theory must indispensably be necessary, because what is truly just and beautiful cannot depend upon chance. What indeed is to be expected from a man, who has no other guide than a long continued practice, and who must of necessity labour under very great uncertainties! Incapable of accounting rationally for what he does, it must be impossible for him to enlighten me, or communicate to me the knowledge which he fancies himself possessed of. How then can I look upon such a man as a master?

SITTING THE HORSE PROPERLY.

Presuming that the horses intended for the use of the army, have been broke, we shall pass over the method of preparing them to be mounted, with the circumstances relating to it.

All soldiers should be instructed to mount and dismount equally well on both sides, which may be of great use in times of hurry and confusion. Place the man in his saddle, with his body rather back, and his head held up with ease, without stiffness; seated neither forwards, nor very backwards, with the breast pushed out a little, and the lower part of the body likewise a little forwards; the thighs and legs turned in without constraint, and the feet in a strait line, neither turned in nor out: By this position, the natural weight of the thighs has a proper and sufficient pressure of itself, and the legs are in readiness to act, when called upon: they must hang down easy and naturally, and be so placed, as not to be wriggling about, touching and tickling the horse's sides, but always near them in case they should be wanted, as well as the heels.

The body must be carefully kept easy and firm, and without any rocking, when in motion; which is a bad habit very easily contracted, especially in galloping. The left elbow must be gently leant against the body, a little forwards; unless it be so rested, the hand cannot be steady,

but

but will be always checking, and consequently have pernicious effects on the horse's mouth.

A firm and well balanced position of the body, on horseback, is of the utmost consequence; as it affects the horse in every motion, and is the best helps; whereas on the contrary, the want of it is the greatest detriment to him, and an impediment in all his actions.

The rider must not bear upon his stirrups, but only let the natural weight of his legs rest on them: for if he bore upon them, he would be raised above, and out of his saddle; which should never be, except in charging sword in hand, with the body inclined forwards at the very instant of attacking. Spurs may be given, as soon as the rider is grown familiar with stirrups, or even long before, if his legs are well placed.

A soldier's right hand should be kept unemployed in riding; it carries the sword, which is a sufficient business for it: In learning therefore to ride, the men should have a whip or switch in it, and hold it upwards, that they may thereby know how to carry their swords properly, keeping it downwards only, when they mount or dismount, that the horse may not be frightened at the sight of it.

A coward and a madman make alike bad riders, and are both alike discovered and confounded by the superior sense of the creature they are mounted upon, who is equally spoilt by both, though in very different ways. The coward, by suffering the animal to have his own way, not only confirms him in his bad habits, but creates new ones in him: and the madman, by false and violent motions and corrections, ruins the horse, and drives him, through despair, into every bad and vicious trick that rage can suggest.

It is very requisite in horsemanship, that the hand and legs should act in correspondence with each other in every thing; the latter always subservient and assistant to the former.

In reining back, the rider should be careful not to use his legs, unless the horse backs on his shoulders; in which case, they must be both applied gently at the same time, and correspond with the hand. If the horse refuse to back at all, the rider's legs must be gently approached, 'till the horse lifts up a leg, as if to go forwards; at which time, when that leg is in the air, the rein of the same side with that leg, which is lifted up, will easily bring that same leg backwards, and accordingly oblige the horse to back: but if the horse offers to rear, the legs must be instantly removed away.

In teaching men a right seat on horseback, the greatest attention must be given to prevent stiffness, and sticking by force in any manner upon any occasion: stiffness disgraces every work; and sticking serves only to throw a man, when displaced, a great distance from his horse, by the spring he must go off with: whereas by a proper equilibrating position of the body, and by the natural weight only of the thighs, he cannot but be firm, and secure in his seat.

No bits should be used, 'till the riders are firm, and the horses bend well to right and left; and then too always with the greatest care and gentleness. The silly custom of using strong and heavy bits, is in all good schools with reason laid aside, as it should be likewise in military riding: they pull down the horse's head, keep it low, thereby obstruct the action of the fore parts, and harden as much the hand of the rider, as mouth of the horse; both which becoming every day more and more insensible together, nothing can be expected but a more unfeeling callousness both in one and the other.

On circles, the rider must lean his body inwards; unless great attention be given to make him do it, he will be perpetually losing his seat outwards, every rapid or irregular motion the horse may make. 'Tis scarce possible for him to be displaced, if he leans his body properly inwards.

Nothing is more ungraceful in itself, more detrimental to a man's seat, or more destructive of the sensibility of a horse's sides, than a continual wriggling unsettledness in a horseman's legs, which prevents the horse from ever going a moment together true, steady, or determined.

The rider's hand is alone always sufficient; and, if it should not, many things should be tried, before so ugly, and bad a resource, as the above-mentioned is thought of; 1st, that of squeezing the thighs; 2d, approaching gently the calves of the legs, and 3d, using the spur; but without distorting the leg, or foot, which a good master will not permit to be done.

OF SUPPLING HORSES, WITH MEN UPON THEM.

When a horse is well prepared and settled in all his motions, and the rider firm, it will be proper then to proceed on towards a farther suppling and teaching both. In regiments,

ments, especially those that are young, there are but very few, if any, tolerable horsemen; which makes the greatest exactness and gentleness absolutely necessary in the instructing of both; but as this part of the subject cannot be properly taught without the assistance of a master, we shall not enter into the minutiæ of it; our intentions being only to convey such general instructions, as may be of occasional use to the young soldier, and to incite in him a desire of being acquainted with the theory, as well as the practical part of his duty.

A horse should never be turned, without first moving a step forwards; an imperceptible motion only of the hand, from one side to the other, is sufficient to turn him. It must also be a constant rule, never to suffer a horse to be stopped, mounted, or dismounted, but when he is well placed.

At first, the figures worked upon must be great, and afterwards made less by degrees, according to the improvement which the man and horse make; and the cadenced pace also, which they work in, must be accordingly augmented. The changes from one side to the other, must be in a bold, determined trot, and at first quite straight forwards, without demanding any side motion on two *pistes*, which it is very necessary to require afterwards, when the horse is sufficiently suppled. By two *pistes* is meant, when the fore parts and hinder parts do not follow, but describe two different lines.

In the beginning, a *longe* is useful on circles, and also on straight lines, to help both the rider and the horse; but afterwards, when they are grown more intelligent, they should go alone. No one, not even the best riders, should ever quite leave off trotting every now and then, in the *longe*, both with, and without stirrups. At the end of the lesson rein back, and then put the horse, by a little at a time, forwards, by approaching both legs gently, and with an equal degree of pressure, to his sides, if necessary, and playing with the bridle: if he rears, push him out immediately into a full trot.

Horses under riders, who use their legs, are, when going to work on two pistes, perpetually setting off with the croup foremost, than which nothing hardly can be worse. It is owing to the leg of the rider being applied to the side of the horse, before the hand has determined the fore parts of the animal, on the line, upon which he is to go.

OF WORKING IN HAND.

Working in hand requires a certain degree of activity, a quick eye, and, like every thing else about horses, good temper, and judgment.

Begin by trotting, then galloping the horse properly, bent inwards by a strap tied from the side ring on the *cavesson* to the ring on the pad. To the head-stall of the longe, a strap and buckle under the throat is very useful to prevent the side part of it from chafing against the eye, which it is very apt to do, when the bending strap is used, and drawn at all tight.

After horses have been a little accustomed to be bent with a strap at the longe, they will very soon longe themselves, as it were; that is to say, that bent with the strap, they will go very well without any longe; and indeed, horses may be brought, with patience and gentleness, to work very well so on almost all lessons in hand.

To explain fully, the method of working in hand; in performing which, two people on foot, are usually employed, would exceed the limits of this Epitome; and which being addressed to young soldiers, rather than riding-masters, we shall only further observe that when it is well done, it has a masterly, active appearance, and is always very useful in suppling and determining horses; but, past all doubt, a good rider mounted, who feels every motion of the horse, must act with more precision, delicacy, and exactness.

OF THE HEAD TO THE WALL, AND OF THE CROUP TO THE WALL.

The difference between the head to the wall, and the croup to the wall, consists in this: in the former, the fore-parts

parts are more remote from the center, and go over more ground; in the latter, the hinder-parts are more remote from the center, and consequently go over more ground: in both, the shoulders must go first.

The motion of the legs in the lesson we are speaking of, to the right, is the same as that of the *epaule en dedans* to the left, and so on the contrary; but the head is always bent and turned differently: in the *epaule en dedans*, the horse looks the contrary way to that which he goes; in this he looks the way he is going.

At the commencement, very little bend must be required; demanding too much at once would perplex the horse, and make him defend himself: it is to be augmented by degrees. If the horse absolutely refuses to obey, it is most probably a sign that either he or his rider has not been sufficiently prepared by previous lessons. It may happen, that weakness, or a hurt in some part of the body, or sometimes temper, though seldom, in the horse, I mean, may be the cause of the horse's defending himself: 'tis the rider's business to find out from whence the obstacle arises, and to remove it; and if he finds it to be from the first mentioned cause, the previous lessons must be resumed again for some time; if from the second, proper remedies must be applied; and if from the last cause, when all fair means that can be tried, have failed, proper corrections, with coolness and judgment, must be used.

In practising this lesson to the right, bend the horse to the right with the right rein, helping the left leg over the right, at the same time when the right leg is just come to the ground, with the left rein crossed towards the right, and keeping the right shoulder back with the right rein towards your body, in order to facilitate the left leg's crossing over the right; and so on the contrary to the left, each rein helping the other by their properly-mixed effects. In working to the right, the rider's left leg helps the hinder parts on to the right, and his right leg stops them, if they get too much so; and so on the contrary to the left; but neither ought to be used, 'till the hand, being employed in a proper manner, has failed, or finds, that a greater force is necessary to bring what is required about, than it can effect alone; for the legs should not only be corresponding with the hand, but also subservient to it; and all unnecessary aids, as well as all force, ought always to be avoided as much as possible. In first beginning to teach this lesson, the croup must be but little constrained; as the horse grows more supple, engage it more by degrees.

In the execution of all lessons, the equilibre of the rider's body is of great use, ease, and help to the horse; it ought always to go with and accompany every motion of the animal; when to the right, to the right; and when to the left, to the left; if it does not, it is a very great hindrance to the horse's going.

This lesson is perpetually of service; for example, in all openings and closings of files; and though it be chiefly employed on straight lines, nevertheless it must be practised, advancing, retreating, turning, &c. as it may be of essential use, almost in all cases whatever: it must be practised too, in all paces, very fast as well as very slow, but of course, gently at first; and changes also from one hand to the other, must frequently be made on two pistes.

Upon all horses, in every lesson and action, it must be observed, that there is no horse but has his own peculiar *appui* or degree of bearing; and also a sensibility of mouth, as likewise a rate of his own, which is absolutely necessary for the rider to discover, and make himself acquainted with. A bad rider always takes off at least the delicacy of both, if not absolutely destroys it, which is generally the case. The horse will inform his rider when he has got his proper bearing in the mouth, by playing pleasantly and steadily with his bit, and by the spray about his chaps. A delicate and good hand will not only always preserve a light *appui*, or bearing in its sensibility, but also of a heavy one, whether naturally so or acquired, make a light one. The lighter this *appui* can be made, the better; but the rider's hand must correspond with it: if it does not, the more the horse is properly prepared, so much the worse for the rider. Instances of this inconvenience of the best of *appuis*, when the rider is not equally taught with the horse, may be seen every day in some gentlemen, who try to get their horses bitted, as they call it, without being suitably prepared themselves for riding them: the consequence of which is, that they ride in danger of breaking their necks: 'till at length, after much hauling about, and by the joint insensibility and ignorance of themselves and their grooms, the poor animals gradually become mere senseless, unfeeling posts, and thereby grow, what they call, settled and pleasant; that is to say, in reality, that they are grown as insensible as their riders, who, because they are void of feeling, and are not firm, must either hold by the bridle, or fall.

To help a horse every now and then, properly, is a very different, and a very useful thing. When the proper *appui* is found, and made of course as light as possible, it must

must not be kept dully fixed without any variation, but be played with; otherwise one equally continued tension of reins, though not a violent one, would render both the rider's hand, and the horse's mouth very dull. The slightest, and frequent giving, and taking, is therefore necessary to keep both perfect.

EVERY soldier must be very well instructed in this lesson of the head and of the tail to the wall: scarce any manœuvre can be well performed without it. In closing and opening of files, it is almost every moment wanted.

WHEN a horse does this lesson on a gallop, the rider must be quiet, and exact in the changes, and be then careful to stop the horse's leg, with which he leads, just at the time when it is most forward, before it comes to the ground, by means of a slight tension of the rein on the same side, which will of course make the other leg go forward, and lead; and, that the horse may change his hinder leg at the same time, which is absolutely necessary, the rider must at the same time cross over his hand, to the left, for example, in changing from the left to the right, replacing it properly the moment the horse has changed both before and behind, which must be done at the same time.

THE TROT.

ALL writers, both ancient and modern, have constantly asserted the trot to be the foundation of every lesson you can teach a horse.

THREE qualities are essentially necessary to make the trot useful. It ought to be extended, supple, and even, or equal. These three qualities are related to, and mutually depend upon each other; in effect, you cannot pass to the supple trot, without having first worked upon the extended trot; and you can never arrive at the even and equal trot, without having first practised the supple. I mean by the extended, that trot, in which the horse trots out without retaining himself, being quite strait, and going directly forwards; this consequently is the kind of trot with which you must begin; for before any thing else

should

should be thought of, the horse should be taught to embrace, and cover his ground readily, and without fear. The trot however may be extended without being supple; for the horse may go directly forward, and yet not have that ease, and suppleness of limb, which distinguishes, and characterises the supple. I define the supple trot to be that, in which the horse at every motion that he makes, bends and plays all his joints, that is to say, those of his shoulders, his knees, and feet, which no colts or raw horses can execute, who have not had their limbs suppled by exercise, and who generally trot with a surprising stiffness, and aukwardness, without the least spring or play in their joints. The even or equal trot, is that wherein the horse makes all his limbs and joints move so equally, and exactly, that his legs never cover more ground one than the other, nor at one time more than another.

To go from the extended trot to the supple, you must gently, and by degrees hold in your horse, and when by exercise he has attained sufficient ease and suppleness to manage his limbs readily, you must insensibly hold him in still more and more, and by degrees you will lead him to the equal trot. The trot is the first exercise to which a horse is put; this is a necessary lesson, but, if given unskilfully, it loses its end, and even does harm. Horses of a hot, and fretful temper, have generally too great a disposition to the extended trot; never abandon these horses to their will; hold them in, pacify them, moderate their motions by retaining them judiciously; their limbs will grow supple, and they will acquire at the same time that union and equality which is so essentially necessary.

AFTER having trotted your horse sufficiently upon a strait line, or directly forwards, work him upon circles; but before you put him to this, walk him gently round the circle, that he may apprehend and know the ground he is to go over. This being done, work him in the trot. A horse that is loaded before, and heavily made, will find more pains and difficulty in uniting his strength, in order to be able to turn, than in going strait forward. The action of turning tries the strength of his reins, and employs his memory and attention; therefore let one part of your lessons be to trot them strait forward: finish them in the same manner, observing that the intervals between the stops, which you should make very often, be long, or short, as you judge necessary.

REINING

REINING BACK—AND OF MOVING FORWARDS IMMEDIATELY AFTER, &c.

Horses, particularly such as are never put in the pillars, nor taught to piaffe, should be reined back a good deal, sometimes slow, sometimes fast, and always without confusion, both in hand, and when rode. Never finish your work by reining back, especially with horses that have any disposition towards retaining themselves; but always move them forwards, and a little upon the haunches also after it, before you dismount; unless they retain themselves very much indeed, in which case nothing at all must be demanded from the haunches, but, quite the contrary, they must immediately be trotted hard out. This lesson of reining back, and piaffing, is excellent to conclude with, and puts a horse well and properly on the haunches: the head and fore-parts must be kept high, and free, for any confinement there destroys action.

That lesson must never be attempted at all, 'till horses are very well suppled, and somewhat accustomed to be put together; otherwise it will have very bad consequences, and create restiveness: infallibly so, if not practised with the utmost exactness and delicacy; and principally with horses, that have the least tendency to retain, or to defend themselves. If they refuse to back, and stand motionless, the rider's legs must be approached with the greatest gentleness to the horse's sides; at the same time as the hand is acting on the reins to solicit the horse's backing. This seldom fails of procuring the desired effect, by raising one of the horse's fore legs, which being in the air, has no weight upon it, and is consequently very easily brought backwards by a small degree of tension in the reins. When this lesson of piaffing is well performed, it is very noble, and useful, and has a pleasing air; it is an excellent one to begin teaching scholars with. In regiments, at their first being raised, when all horses are brought in young and raw, there can of course be no horses ready prepared in it for this purpose; but a little time and diligence remedies this inconvenience.

TO MAKE HORSES STAND FIRE, &c.

In order that horses may stand fire, the sound of drums, and all sorts of different noises, you must use them to it by degrees, in the stable, at feeding-time; and instead of being frightened at it, they will soon come to like it, as a signal for eating.

With respect to such horses as are afraid of burning objects, begin by keeping them still, at a certain distance from some lighted straw: caress the horse, and in proportion as his fright diminishes, approach gradually the burning straw very gently, and increase the size of it. By this means he will very quickly be brought to be so familiar with it, as to walk undaunted even through it. The same method and gentleness must be observed also, in regard to glittering arms, colours, standards, &c.

As to those horses that are apt to lie down in the water, if animating them, and attacking them vigorously, should fail of the desired effect, then break a straw-bottle full of water upon their heads, the moment they begin to lie down, and let the water run into their ears, which is a thing they apprehend very much, and which will in all probability soon cure them of the trick.

All troop-horses must be taught to stand quiet and still when they are shot off from, to stop the moment you present, and not to move after firing, 'till they are required to do it; this lesson ought especially to be observed in light troops, and in should never be neglected in any kind of cavalry whatsoever: in short, the horses must be taught to be so cool and undisturbed, as to suffer the riders to act upon them with the same freedom, as if they were on foot. Patience, coolness, and temper, are the only means requisite for accomplishing this end. The rider, when he fires, must be very attentive not to throw himself forwards too much, or otherwise *derange* himself in his seat. Begin by walking the horse gently, then stop and keep him from stirring for some time, so as to accustom him by degrees not to have the least idea of moving without orders: if he does, back him; and when you stop him, and he is quite still, leave the reins quite loose, and caress him.

To

To use a horse to fire-arms, first put a pistol or carbine in the manger with his feed; then use him to the sound of the lock and the pan; after which, when you are upon him, shew the piece to him, presenting it forwards, sometimes on one side, sometimes on the other: when he is thus far reconciled, proceed to flash in the pan; after which, put a small charge into the piece, and so continue augmenting it by degrees to the quantity which is commonly used: if he seems uneasy, walk him forwards a few steps slowly, and then stop, back, move forwards, then stop again, and caress him. Great care must be taken not to burn, or singe the horse any where in firing; he would remember it, and be very shy, for a long time. Horses are also often disquieted and unsteady at the clash and glittering of arms, at the drawing and returning of swords, all which they must be familiarized to, by frequency and gentleness.

TO LEARN HORSES TO LEAP OVER DITCHES, &c.

In going over rough and bad ground, the men must keep their hands high, and their bodies back.

It is very expedient for cavalry in general, but particularly for light cavalry, that their horses should be very ready and expert in leaping over ditches, hedges, gates, &c. not only singly but in squadrons, and lines. The leaps, of whatever sort they are, which the horses are brought to in the beginning, ought to be very small ones, and as the horse improves in his leaping, be augmented by degrees; for if the leaps were increased considerably at once, the horse would blunder, grow fearful, and contract an aukward way of leaping with hurry, and confusion. The riders must keep their bodies back, raise their hand a little in order to help the fore-parts of the horse up, and be very attentive to their equilibre, without raising themselves up in the saddle, or moving their arms.

Let the ditches and hedges, &c. you first bring the horses to, be inconsiderable; and in this, as in every thing else, let the increafe be made by degrees. Accuftom them to come up gently to every thing, which they are to leap over, and to ftand coolly at it for fome time; and then to raife themfelves gently, up, and go clear over it, without either floth or hurry. When they leap well ftanding, then ufe them to walk gently up to the leap, and to go over it without firft halting at it; and after that practice is familiar to them, repeat the like in a gentle trot, and fo by degrees fafter and fafter, 'till at length it is as familiar to them to leap flying on a full gallop, as any other way; all which is to be acquired with great facility by calm and foft means, without any hurry.

TO ACCUSTOM HORSES TO SWIM.

Horses fhould alfo be accuftomed to fwim, which often may be neceffary upon fervice; and if the men and horfes both are not ufed to it, both may be frequently liable to perifh in the water. A very fmall portion of ftrength is fufficient to guide a horfe, any where indeed, but particularly in the water, where they muft be permitted to have their heads, and be as little conftrained as poffible in any fhape. In croffing rivers, the horfe's head fhould be kept againft the current, more or lefs, according to the fituation of the place, higher up, or lower down, purpofed to land at, and the degree of rapidity of the water. In going down the ftream, the ftraighter the horfe is the better. The rider had always better quit his ftirrups on thefe occafions, for fear of accidents, and his getting entangled in them. A horfe is turned difficultly in the water; it muft be done very gently and carefully.

TO CURE RESTIVENESSES, &C.

Previous to any mention of the different kinds of reftiveneffes, vices, and defences, &c. it is not amifs to obferve, that a horfe's being good or ill-natured, greatly depends on

the

the temper of the perfon, that is put about him, efpecially at firft, and confequently one cannot be too careful and watchful in this point.

WHENEVER a horfe makes refiftance, one ought, before a remedy or correction is thought of, to examine very minutely all the tackle about him, if any thing hurts or tickles him, whether he has any natural or accidental weaknefs, or in fhort any the leaft impediment in any part. For want of this precaution, and previous infpection, many fatal, and often irreparable difafters happen: the poor dumb animal is frequently accufed falfely of being reftive and vicious; is ufed ill without reafon, and being forced into defpair, is, in a manner, obliged to act accordingly, be his temper and inclination ever fo well difpofed. It muft never be forgot, that it is neceffary to work on the minds of horfes, at firft by flow motions which give time to reflect.

IT is very feldom the cafe, that a horfe is really, and by nature vicious; but if fuch be found, chaftifements will become neceffary fometimes, but they muft then be always made ufe of with the greateft judgment and temper. The propriety of aids is to forefee, and prevent faults. The propriety of chaftifements is to correct them.

CORRECTION, according as you ufe it, throws a horfe into more or lefs violent action, which, if he be weak, he cannot fupport: but a vicious ftrong horfe is to be confidered in a very different light, being able both to undergo and confequently to profit by all leffons; and is, in every refpect, far preferable to the beft-natured weak one upon earth. Patience and fcience are never-failing means to reclaim a wicked horfe: in whatfoever manner he defends himfelf, bring him back frequently with gentlenefs, but with firmnefs too, to the leffon which he feems moft averfe to. Horfes are by degrees made obedient through the hope of recompence and the fear of punifhment: how to mix thefe two motives judicioufly together is a very difficult matter, not eafy to be prefcribed; it requires much thought and practice; and not only a good head, but a good heart likewife.

PLUNGING is a very common defence among reftive and vicious horfes: if they do it in the fame place or backing, they muft by the rider's legs, and fpurs too, fometimes firmly applied, be obliged to go forwards, and their heads kept up high. But if they do it flying forwards, keep them back, ride them gently and very flow for a good while together, and back them gently every now and then. Of all bad tempers and qualities in horfes, thofe, which

are

are occasioned by harsh treatment and ignorant riders, which are very common, are the worst.

Rearing is a bad vice, and in weak horses especially, a very dangerous one. Whilst the horse is up, the rider must yield his hand, and when the horse is descending he must vigorously determine him forwards, by approaching his legs to the horse's sides: if this be done at any other time, but whilst the horse is coming down, it may add a spring to his rearing, and make him fall backwards. With a good hand on them, horses seldom persist in this vice; for they are themselves naturally much afraid of falling backwards. If this method, which I have mentioned, fails, which it scarcely ever will, you must make the horse kick up behind, by getting somebody on foot to strike or prick him behind.

Starting often proceeds from a defect in the sight, which therefore must be carefully looked into. Whatever the horse is afraid of, bring him up to it gently; if you caress him every step he advances, he will go quite up to it by degrees, and soon grow familiar with all sorts of objects. Nothing but great gentleness can correct this fault: for if you inflict punishment, the apprehension of chastisement becomes prevalent, and causes more starting, than the fear of the object. If you let him go by the object, without bringing him up to it, you increase the fault and confirm him in his fears.

I have often heard people maintain, some, that blows are necessary to cure this evil; and others, that horses should be suffered to have their own way in it, but I cannot help saying, that I think both equally in the wrong.

Quarrelling with horses, plaguing, or beating them, as one often sees done, not only spoils both their tempers, and their paces, but it teaches them to trip, stumble, fall, start, run away, and to be unsteady and vicious, &c. whilst gentleness and coolness would very soon bring them to go through, or over any bad place whatever, with ease, good-humour and safety. Beat a horse for a trip, or such a kind of thing, and he will soon do it again through fear and hurry. Such failures sometimes proceed from weakness. In that case, proper food, and gentle exercise, by restoring the animal to health, and vigour, will cure him of them. If they come from inattention, or from the badness of his paces, he must have a good rider to render him attentive, and mend his movements.

FARRIERY,

FARRIERY, &c.

We shall not enter on the many systems of Farriery, or of Shoeing, with the several particulars attacked thereto, as the Treatises on those subjects are many, and most of them generally known. However it may not be amiss to quote a few passages from the Earl of Pembroke on those heads.

The methods of treating and keeping horses are as various, and for the generality as inconsistent with reason, as those of shoeing are; but a little consideration would, in most common cases, at least direct people right in both. One pampers his cattle, with a view of strengthening them; and afterwards, by way of correction, he pours down drugs into them without thought or measure; another lets no air at all in his stable; from whence his horses inevitably catch cold, when they stir out of it, and are rotted, if they stay in it, by bad corrupted air: a third, equally wise, leaves his stable open, and his cattle exposed to the wind and weather at all times, whether his horses or the weather be hot or cold, and frequently even in wind drafts, whilst they are in a sweat. All these different notions and practices are alike attended with destruction to horses; as also are the many extravagancies that prevail in the same contradictory extremes, with regard to coverings. But in answer to all these foolish systems, reason plainly suggests to us, that proper wholesome food, a well tempered circulation of sweet air, moderate and constant exercise, with due care, and suitable cloathing, as weather and occasions may require, will never fail to preserve horses sound and in health.

Upon service, the allowance of all kinds of forage, whenever there is a possibility of supplying it, is sufficient; but sometimes it cannot be procured for a long while together: besides which misfortune, it is very often most shamefully and carelessly wasted; not to mention, that commissaries in general seldom furnish out the due quantity or quality of any thing, which they have agreed and engaged for, and are most amply paid for.

At home, our horses are crammed and ruined with over-much hay, and the allowance of corn is scanty. A kind of mill, not to grind corn, but only just to crack and bruise it a little, is so useful, that no regiment should ever march without one. Every grain of it goes to nourishment; none is to be found in the dung; and three feeds of it go further than four as commonly given, which have not been in the mill. Cut wheaten straw, and a little hay too sometimes mixed with it, is excellent food: to a quartern of corn put the same quantity of cut straw, and now and then, if a horse is very lean, but not otherwise, about half a one of hay, and let them all be well mingled together; and as chopped straw is generally exceedingly dry, sprinkle a little water upon the feed in the manger. This proportion of chopped straw may seem great, but considering the lightness of it, it is not such in reality. It obliges horses to chew their meat, and is many other ways of use.

No trimming with scissars should be permitted; but whatever rough hairs appear, should be taken off by dressing. The inside particularly of the ears should never be trimmed, but always kept clean: nature has placed hairs within them for reasons very obvious: when they are cut away, dust and insects frequently get into the ears, incommode horses very much, and sometimes cause a serious ailment in those parts.

A COMMON complaint among troop-horses is broken wind, which is chiefly occasioned by stuffing them with too much hay; and often by hurrying them too violently after drinking, and after their coming at first from grass. There is no sovereign remedy for broken-wind; but the greatest palliative I know of, is lime-water, which is oftener of service, if continued long, or rather always indeed, than any other remedy I know of, owing probably not only to the good effects of the lime, but also to the small quantity of liquid the horses take; for very few will ever drink plentifully of this water, and many will go several days without drinking at all, before they will even taste it.

SHOEING.

'Tis strange, that there should be so many ridiculous and absurd methods of shoeing, when it is so manifest, that
a small

a small share of common sense, with a moment's reflection upon the structure of a horse's foot, cannot but suggest the proper one. Frequent removals of shoes are detrimental, and tear the foot, but sometimes they are very necessary: this is an inconvenience, which half-shoes are liable to, though excellent in several other respects; for the end of the shoe being very short, is apt to work soon into the foot, and consequently must then be moved. Soldiers should always carry two spare shoes with them, on the upper end and outward side of each holster pipe, with some nails. Some should carry a hammer, others a pair of pinchers, others a butteris, and all be taught how to fix on a shoe. The weight of these things, properly divided, is trifling. The use of them would be soon found on service, particularly with light troops, and on detachments, where farriers cannot be present.

Mr. CLARKE, in his excellent treatise upon shoeing and feet, insists, that oil, greasy stuffings, and ointments, agree but with few horses; that they stop the natural perspiration, and that frequent washings with water, moisture, and coolness, keep them in a much more perfect state. The experience I have had, since I saw his book, convinces me that he is right in general: the natural and superior benefit which feet and hoofs receive at grass, from the dew, rains and moisture of the earth, is a proof of it; and on the other hand we see, that race-horses, particularly at New-Market, where they are always exercised on a dry, close turf, and where they drink out of troughs, round which there is no water for them to stand in, are subject to a variety of diseases in the feet, and hoofs, though they are kept constantly greased.

MISCELLANEOUS REMARKS.

It is a common custom to give walking exercise to horses who have sprains, which is very pernicious; they should not be stirred at all, if possible: absolute rest is the best remedy for them.

f A BLANKET

A BLANKET for each man, carried under the saddle, is of vast use to the horse's back, as well as to the man, on many occasions. Every man should have one.

EVERY troop ought to have a cutting-box belonging to it, and one man constantly employed in camp all day at it, in chopping hay, straw, &c. It is very easily carried about.

FORAGE, whatever it is, must not be cut too long, nor very short, but of such a length, that it may not, from its lightness, be blown up the horse's nostrils, out of the nose-bag, or canvass trough. A lazy fellow at the cutting-box, if not watched, is very apt, by way of getting rid of his work soon, to cut it much too long.

THE Germans wisely carry, upon all occasions whatever, every man a double feed of chopped straw and corn mixed together which is never touched, but by express order of the commanding officer, and then too in such quantities, and at what time he thinks fit to direct. It frequently happens upon long marches, and even sometimes when the troops stand still, that forage cannot be procured for some days together; then this practice, which I have just mentioned, in a short time gives strong and apparent proofs of its utility, by the preservation of their horses good plight. It is the means of saving the lives of many horses, and helps, in cases of exigencies, to keep up the vigour of most of them. None but those, who have been eye-witnesses to the fact, can tell what harm a deficiency of forage, only for two days, does horses, especially in marches by night, and in bad weather: some are often disabled by it for the whole campaign, and some for ever after.

CURSORY HINTS on TACTICS;

SELECTED FROM GENERAL LLOYD, MR. SAXE, MR. SIMES, AND OTHERS.

To the respectable opinions we have given, concerning the defence of the nation, together with those on military horsemanship, we will now beg leave to add a few on tactics. We shall not trespass on the patience of the reader, by pointing out what we conceive to be a proper Military Discipline; or, by giving a comparison between the various systems that prevail in the several European nations; the nature of our work confining us to general observations only.

DISCIPLINE.

NOTHING can be so necessary to the soldier as discipline: without it, troops may become more dangerous than useful, more hurtful to ourselves, than our enemies. The means of discipline are regulated by our military laws, and by the articles of war; which command obedience to superiors; and courage against an enemy: in regard to private conversation, politeness should exceed authority, and the officer subside in the gentleman.

THE nature of the service is such, that in actions, errors cannot be committed with impunity. The particulars necessary to be observed, are many and various; but none more essential to victory, than a strict obedience to orders, and a just observation to signals: On this depends the success and safety of the troops.

It is is a FALSE NOTION, *that* SUBORDINATION, *and* A PASSIVE OBEDIENCE TO SUPERIORS, *is any* DEBASEMENT *of* A MAN'S COURAGE. *So far from it,* THAT IT IS A GENERAL REMARK,

REMARK, *that those armies who have been* SUBJECT *to the* SEVEREST DISCIPLINE, *have* ALWAYS *performed the* GREATEST ACTIONS.

NEW MODE OF FORMING A LINE.

I HUMBLY propose that the infantry be ranged *four* deep; that the *fourth* rank be armed with a *pike, eleven or twelve feet long*; two feet of which must be made of steel, two inches broad, to cut on each side, without any hatchet, or cross bar, that it may easily pass through the *hedges*. This fourth rank must be composed of the tallest and strongest men.

THIS formation of the line, will render it less extensive, stronger, and much more active; is proper for every operation; and *is particularly adapted to our country*, every where inclosed with hedges and ditches. In a plain, no INFANTRY, *formed in the usual manner, can resist its shocks an instant, or even approach your line;* much less, if this is placed behind an entrenchment or hedge. Besides, if you form a battalion or two into squares, protected by some howitzers on the flanks, no cavalry, however brave, can overturn them. The three first ranks, protected by a row of pikes, which project before them at least five feet, will feel the advantage; and soon find their superiority, in whatever ground they are attacked, as well as in attacking the enemy. Let an experiment be made, the event will shew the superiority of the method I propose, over that now in practice. It is a novelty. Very true; and this novelty will not a little disconcert the enemy.

NEW ORDER OF BATTLE.

THE order of battle now adopted in Europe, is defective and absurd. The infantry and cavalry formed three deep, make the line so very extensive, that it loses all its activity, which is the soul of military manœuvres, and alone can insure success. In the manner our line is now formed, not a third of the army is engaged, and that successively; so that numbers

numbers are of no use, and only serve to retard its motions, and increase the expence. To remedy these defects, I would humbly propose, that all the infantry be formed in such a manner, that between each battalion, or regiment, an interval of 150 yards be left. Behind these intervals, I would have the cavalry placed in two lines, at a proper distance, each squadron seperately, with intervals to manœuvre upon.

By this you could extend your line to any length, without any danger, and bring the whole into action at once. And though the enemy be double in number, you may outflank him, and are in reality stronger than him; for you attack his whole front with superior forces. Besides, the motions of the whole line are more rapid, as each regiment or battalion acts by itself. If your line is broken in some places, the enemy cannot avail himself of the disorder, before your cavalry advances, and gives the infantry time to recover. If your infantry breaks that of the enemy in any point, then advance your left line of cavalry to attack and disperse it; the whole moving rapidly, a general slaughter ensues, and your victory is complete and decisive.

I once saw 7 or 8000 foot, that were so imprudent to break their line, to attack an advanced battalion; and they were defeated and dispersed, by 300 horse, in a few minutes. Another advantage of this order of battle, is, that it is general, and equally adapted to every species of country; and, as it is peculiarly adapted to this country, I hope it will be received and applied on the present occasion.

As to cavalry, it must never appear but in the moment it is brought into action, action being the very essence of cavalry.

OF MUSIC.

The philosophic General, Marshal Saxe observes, that, deprive an army of music, and the most indefatigable among them, will not be able on a march to bear it for two hours. By means of music, you will always be able to regulate your pace at pleasure; your rear can never lag behind, and the whole will stop with the same foot. Your wheelings will be performed with celerity and grace. Your men's legs will never mix together. You will not be obliged to halt,

perhaps

perhaps in the middle of every wheel to recover the step; nor will the men be fatigued in any degree equal to what they are at present.

This sufficiently proves that sounds have a secret power over us, disposing our organs to bodily exercises, and at the same time, deluding, as it were, the toil of them. All airs in common or triple time, will produce such an effect. The movement by music is so natural, that it can hardly be ever avoided. I have frequently taken notice, that in beating to arms, the soldiers have fallen into the ranks in cadence, without being sensible of it, nature and instinct carrying them involuntary; besides, without music, it is impossible in close order to perform any evolution.

OF CAVALRY.

The cavalry ought to be well appointed, to be mounted on horses inured to fatigue; to be incumbered with as little baggage as possible; but above all, that leading mistake of making the horses fat should be avoided. The oftener likewise they see an enemy, the better; as it renders them familiar with danger, and capable of attempting any thing. But that immoderate love we are apt to have for the horses, leaves us ignorant of their real power and importance.

I had a regiment of German horse in Poland, says M. Saxe, with which I marched in 18 months above 4,500 miles. I can also affirm that at the end of that time, it was fitter for service, than another whose horses were too full of flesh. Unless cavalry be able to endure fatigue, in running and violent exercises, they are in reality good for nothing. But they must be broke by degrees, and familiarized to it in length of time by custom; after which gallopping at full speed by squadrons, and a constant use of violent exercises, will both preserve them in better condition, and make them last much longer. It will likewise form the men, and give them a martial and becoming air.

An army unprovided with light horse, or not having a sufficient number to oppose against those of the enemy, may be compared to a man armed *cap à pié*, who is to encounter a troop of school-boys, without any other offensive weapons than clods of earth. This Hercules will presently be obliged to retire, struggling for want of breath, and confounded with shame.

TO HARRASS AN INVADING ARMY ON ITS MARCH.

A PARTIZAN of enterprize and spirit, with 3 or 400 men, will find means to attack an army on its march in a defile, and to accasion a great deal of disorder and inconvenience; at the close of the day, if he seize an opportunity to cut off the enemy's baggage, he will be able to carry away a considerable part of it, without exposing himself to much danger. For if he retreats between two passes, and makes a vigorous opposition in his rear, he will thereby check all pursuit. In case he is hard pressed, he can march, all along by the side of the carriages, and the first house he finds, he may there oblige the invading army to make a sudden halt; during which time the baggage that he has taken from them is marching on apace.

THE DENSITY, OR CLOSENESS OF A BODY OF TROOPS.

THE more closely united and compact the constituent parts of a physical body are, the more solid and dense that body is said to be. This term has been applied to the troops, and many persons take it to be literally true. From hence it has been imagined the closeness or density of a body of troops cannot be too great, and that its strength increases in proportion to its density. This mistake arises from an expression foreign to the object, and which implies more than was first intended; for were soldiers so closely united in rank and files as to form but one lump or mass, the troops would become a mere lifeless passive body, incapable of performing any action. A body of forces should be then more or less closely united, according to the weapons they are to use: but whatever the nature of their weapons may be, they should have their bodies and hands free, that nothing may lessen their quantity of action.

OF A RETREAT.

THIS sort of disposition is never made with so much care as that of advancing. In this the rear is exposed, which is
always

always very dangerous to do. Besides, all men in a retreat, contract a degree of fear, which in a manner reduces them to the state of being half defeated. This circumstance is difficult to be accounted for otherwise, than by ascribing it to the natural imbecillity of the human heart. Therefore the retreat of an enemy in a strange country, is generally followed by a total defeat, where the country is close and full of defiles.

OF ENGLISH COURAGE.

It is a great defect, says M. Saxe, in any infantry to be capable of acting only in certain dispositions. This opinion will certainly meet with opposition: but I doubt much if we have many generals so enterprizing as to undertake to march, in an open plain, a body of infantry, in sight of a numerous cavalry, and to flatter themselves that they could be able to maintain their ground for several hours, with 15 or 20 battalions, in the midst of an army; *as the English did at Fontenoy, without either throwing away their fire, or even altering their countenance, notwithstanding all the attacks* THE CAVALRY *could make upon them.*

These are things we have all seen; but self-love forbids the mention of it, because we, speaking of the French, well know OUR INCAPACITY TO IMITATE THEM.

REMARKS.

THUS have we given the remarks of some great characters, on the interesting subject of INVASION, and on some useful points of Tactics, as connected with the best modes of defence, on such an occasion. Our object, throughout this work, has been to shew, from the examples of past times, and from the opinions of distinguished men, that although invasions may be often menaced, and sometimes attempted, yet they can never succeed, IF THE NATION BE ARMED, *and the* GREAT BODY *of* THE PEOPLE *are determined* TO PRESERVE THEIR FREEDOM, *from* SECRET TREACHERY, *and* OPEN HOSTILITY.

THE END.

www.ingramcontent.com/pod-product-compliance
Lightning Source LLC
Chambersburg PA
CBHW020756230426
43666CB00007B/719